LIVING THE CALL

Praise for *Living the Call*

Every Christian has the right and duty to participate in the Church's evangelical mission to spread the Gospel of the Kingdom of God. Simon and Novak explain why, and how, that mission can be lived today.

—George Weigel, Distinguished Senior Fellow,
Ethics and Public Policy Center

Nothing can advance the Kingdom of God more than Christians getting out of the pews and into the world. *Living the Call* is an inspiring guide to do just that.

—Chuck Colson, Founder, Prison Fellowship and the
Chuck Colson Center for Christian Worldview

Living the Call inspires readers with particular stories of ordinary yet heroic virtue, while guiding us to further participation in that which is good and noble. It is uplifting and practical.

—Edwin Feulner, President, The Heritage Foundation

Bill Simon and Michael Novak show us how laypeople are fulfilling their baptismal call: to bring Christ to the world. Some do this within Church structures, most in the public square. I found their concluding account of the spiritual resources which support this call riveting.

—Fr. John Jay Hughes, Author, *No Ordinary
Fool: A Testimony to Grace*

LIVING THE CALL
AN INTRODUCTION TO THE LAY VOCATION

*Michael Novak
and William E. Simon Jr.*

ENCOUNTER BOOKS NEW YORK • LONDON

First American edition published in 2011 by Encounter Books,
an activity of Encounter for Culture and Education, Inc.,
a nonprofit, tax exempt corporation.
Encounter Books website address: www.encounterbooks.com

Manufactured in the United States and printed on
acid-free paper. The paper used in this publication meets
the minimum requirements of ANSI/NISO Z39.48 1992
(R 1997) (*Permanence of Paper*).

FIRST AMERICAN EDITION

LIBRARY OF CONGRESS CATALOGING-IN-PUBLICATION DATA

Novak, Michael.
Living the call: an introduction to the lay vocation/
by Michael Novak and William E. Simon, Jr.
p. cm.
Includes bibliographical references and index.
ISBN-13: 978-1-59403-586-9 (hardcover: alk. paper)
ISBN-10: 1-59403-586-5 (hardcover: alk. paper) 1. Lay ministry—Catholic
Church. I. Simon, William E., 1951- II. Title.
BX1920.N69 2011
253.088'282—dc22

2011001701

CONTENTS

PART II: THE SEARCH WITHIN

For my wife, Cindy, a constant source
of respect, admiration, and love.
—Bill

For Karen Laub-Novak, Artist of the
Dark Night, fun-loving and carrier of joy.
—Michael

A WORD FROM BILL

Thirty years ago, if you had told me I was going to write a book about opportunities for lay Catholics to become more involved in the Church, I would have chuckled and said, "Not likely" or maybe, more emphatically, "Highly unlikely."

I grew up the oldest of seven children in an Irish Catholic family, going to church every Sunday. I even had a sort of evangelical experience while I was working at a hospital during high school. But my young adulthood, which I sometimes jokingly refer to as my "George W. Bush phase," was not a model of religious piety. I worked hard, but I did a lot of partying too. I got married at 27 and was divorced by the time I was 32.

I still have some trouble piecing together how I got so lost in my 20s. But slowly, I returned to the Church. After an annulment, I remarried, and though my wife didn't convert to Catholicism until 15 years later, we raised our three children in the Catholic faith. My churchgoing and sacramental life became consistent—it had a niche in my life. I juggled a career and a family, and on Sundays, we would go to Mass. Occasionally, I would yearn for greater spiritual engagement, but that feeling would usually disappear amid the busyness of life.

But about a dozen years ago, with some significant professional and material success under my belt, I began to feel that something was missing, that maybe these three things in my life—my family, my faith, and my career—shouldn't be separate. And maybe the balance among the three wasn't quite right.

So I started to pray.

I had this soft inkling, no great thunderbolt, that God wanted me to become more involved in the Church, even to speak or preach there or to be of service in some way. The message seemed to come out of nowhere. The extent of my involvement in church until that time had been to sit in the pews and help with fundraising. But a little voice kept pushing me. So I thought, Okay, I'll go down this path a little bit. So I did some research. I consulted with my pastor, Monsignor Lloyd Torgerson, as well as some other friends and acquaintances. And I even did some reading in canon law. What I found surprised me: there was nothing in Catholic doctrine that should prevent me from speaking in church, except custom, as long as certain rules were observed. Moreover, I discovered there were plenty of opportunities to become involved in daily parish life, partly because of, no doubt, the decline in vocations.

Maybe, just maybe, this inkling had some substance to it.

As part of my due diligence, I went to talk to an old friend of my father's, Michael Novak. His kindness and his enthusiasm about the idea of greater lay involvement in the Church led to what, for me, has become a life-changing dialogue. We talked about the future of the Church and all the difficulties it faces in the coming years. The internal crises standing before the Church—including the steep decline in the number of clergy—and the external pressures from an increasingly secular society are going to make the 21st century a challenging one. But my conversations with Michael made me hopeful about the future of the Catholic Church and about the opportunities for laypeople to deepen their faith, both from an interior and exterior perspective.

In the years since Michael and I first discovered the common interest we had in encouraging lay vocations, we both became sidetracked with other projects. Then last year, we met again and were reminded of that original spark of an idea.

I was grateful to have the opportunity to revisit this subject—both to reflect on it personally and to pursue a systematic study of the lay vocations.

It became clear as I began the research for this book that there had been dramatic developments regarding lay participation in the 10 years since Michael and I first spoke, all of them consistent with the promise of the Second Vatican Council. Reading the statement by the United States Conference of Catholic Bishops, "Co-Workers in the Vineyard of the Lord," it was impossible not to be excited about and inspired by the broad varieties of opportunities for laypeople:

> All of the baptized are called to work toward the transformation of the world. Most do this by working in the secular realm; some do this by working in the Church and focusing on the building of ecclesial communion, which has among its purposes the transformation of the world. Working in the Church is a path of Christian discipleship to be encouraged by the hierarchy. The possibility that laypersons undertake Church ministries can be grounded in Scripture and the teachings of the Church, from St. Paul to the Second Vatican Council and in more recent documents. "Sharing in the function of Christ, priest, prophet and king, the laity have an active part of their own in the life and activity of the Church. Their activity within the Church communities is so necessary

that without it the apostolate of the pastors will frequently be unable to obtain its full effect." (*Lumen Gentium*, n. 33)

Today in parishes, schools, Church institutions, and diocesan agencies, laity serve in various "ministries, offices, and roles" that do not require sacramental ordination but rather "find their foundation in the Sacraments of Baptism and Confirmation, indeed, for a good many of them, in the Sacrament of Matrimony." (*Christifideles Laici,* n. 23)

The impact of these words hit me hard because the meaning was unmistakable. The days of "pray, pay, and obey" were over.

More roles were being offered to laypeople. Our Church understood how the talents of laypeople could be put to good use whether in the parish, in Catholic schools, or in myriad other places, helping others in matters of administering the affairs of the organization.

There is so much energy among the laypeople I have met— and so much untapped potential. My own father became a Eucharistic minister at age 65. I saw firsthand the great fulfillment it brought him. And I wondered why he didn't start sooner. I think he would say he wished he had but that he was too busy with his career and his family. And I wondered if other people might feel the same way or simply do not realize how much they could gain by getting more involved in the life of the Church.

In my parish of Saint Monica's near Los Angeles, I have seen firsthand the lay leadership in our high school, in the parish business affairs, and in a majority of the 69 ministries that are presently on offer. I have been a member of the finance council for many years, together with other parishioners who help oversee the finances in collaboration with our pastor.

A few years ago in that capacity, I met Bob Buford, a successful businessman and the author of a book called *Halftime,* devoted to helping middle-age people do something significant with their lives. He likes to talk about how when you're younger, you want to devote 80 percent of your time to your job and your family and 20 percent of your time to other things. But slowly, the priorities start to shift as you get older. Your 40s and 50s, he says, are the "bridge years." Bob calls this transition "going from success to significance."

Well, I'm 59 now, so I guess you could say I've come to this shift a little bit later than many. My wife says I shouldn't beat myself up over it.

But now I'm ready to cross that bridge. I don't feel like I should devote the bulk of the rest of my life to getting a greater return on my financial investments. I want to make a positive difference in people's lives. I have found a calling. And if this book can help others do the same, well, I'll thank God for that.

A WORD FROM MICHAEL

In the fall of 1963, just after we were married, my wife, Karen, and I took a ship to Rome to be present at the Second Vatican Council, which was about to open its Second Session (of four). Karen wanted to create a series of prints on the Apocalypse of St. John. My aim was to pay our way by writing articles first and, with luck, to accumulate enough material to write a report on the Second Session such as the layman Lord Acton had published about the First Vatican Council.

For laypersons in the Church, it was rapidly becoming a heady time. Suddenly, we were accorded (even by priests and bishops) uncommon respect and attention. The "new" and the "relevant" ascended in authority. The "traditional" and the "authoritative" seemed in decline.

After I published my book *The Open Church*, about the proceedings of the Second Vatican Council, I was often invited to speak and to write on "The New Layman" or "Dissent in the Church"—in which I was not so much promoting dissent as pointing out its utility, even necessity, in coming to ever-nearer approximations to the truth of things. I was asked to address

"The Role of the Laity." Oh yes, also, "The People of God"—then the new, preferred way of saying "Church." The Church is not just the hierarchy; it is the whole people.

The French philosopher Étienne Gilson wittily pointed out that it is not good for the Church to have too many really good popes in a row; such good fortune tended to create a top-down dependency. Now and then, he wrote tongue-in-cheek, a bad pope—a scandal-ridden pope—was a blessing for the Church. For it reminded all that ours is a Church of sinners and that our faith's dependence is not on the morals of our clergy but on the unshakable fidelity of God to us.

Witnessing the birth of the new role of laypersons in the Church, their new eminence and recognized responsibility in their own vast domain, affected me permanently. I have remained interested in the ups and downs of the past turbulent decades of changes in the life and role of laypersons in the Church.

A decade ago, when Bill Simon challenged me to turn my attention to this theme, it seemed like a providential invitation. After all, a little more than 25 years ago, Bill's father, William E. Simon Sr., had invited me to participate in one of the most striking lay initiatives of all time. The Catholic bishops of the United States announced a new project for their National Conference: a study of the American economy in connection with the Catholic faith. For those of us passionately interested in engaging the whole Church in a fresh study of economics, especially the new kind of economy pioneered by the United States as nowhere else, this announcement was a godsend. We cheered the idea. If the Catholic bishops had addressed the Catholics of the United States in 1934, they would have had to address them as "poor." How did it happen that when they published their letter "Economic Justice for All" in 1984, they addressed their fellow Catholics as "affluent"? How did the transformation from "poor" to "affluent" happen so quickly?

In the new lay spirit, we could not help noticing that the field of economics is primarily the responsibility of laypeople, not that of the clergy (although, of course, the economy affects their responsibilities too). The Second Vatican Council had encouraged lay participation, even initiative and leadership, in such worldly matters. So we did our duty. We undertook writing our own lay letter, not to interfere with the draft the bishops were preparing, and hopefully not to contradict it, but to expand and deepen its worldly range. We suggested, for example, more attention to the question of how new wealth is created and more attention to the main cause of poverty in the U.S.: households of many children headed by women without husbands.

Even in that time, we could not help but consider the chutzpah of the thing. No other Catholic laypersons in the world had ever taken it upon themselves to address their own "pastoral letter" (so to speak) to the world. But given the recent developments, one would have thought that this deed would be widely recognized as a beautiful fulfillment of the Council's express hopes for a new burst of lay responsibility. We did not claim to speak for all laypersons nor all lay points of view. No one could do that in so pluralistic a land as ours. We proposed our letter as something quite new, a lay initiative in a field in which the like had never been seen. It would have been satisfying to see other groups of laypersons, with different economic views, put their heads together and issue their own statements. Instead, there was a certain amount of carping about ours.

Before publishing our letter, we consulted with Archbishop Rembert Weakland, the head of the bishops' committee on this project, about when he would like us to release our draft. We had sent him a copy as soon as we finished. I suggested that we publish our letter first, so there could be no question of our public dissent (if it turned out that the two drafts were significantly at odds, which we did not really expect but had no way of judging). The archbishop thought on it and then agreed.

Soon after our letter appeared, our lay commission was accused of a "pre-emptive strike" on the bishops' letter. This, of course, was simply not true. We had been perfectly willing to wait a week or a month. But the very accusation suggested to many that our letter must have been quite effective, and in some ways more arresting than that of the bishops.

In the quarter-century that has elapsed since the dispute over that letter, the push and pull between the laity and the clergy has continued apace. Laypersons were empowered and encouraged by the Second Vatican Council. Even beginning in the 1940s, the record of lay movements around the world—in labor unions, in Christian democratic parties, in Catholic Youth and Catholic Family movements, and in Catholic Action of many sorts, in movements among lay women, such as in Grailville, Ohio—was quite impressive. But after the Council ended in 1965, and especially during the past 10 years, lay activities took off with a woosh!

So why should we be giving this subject more serious consideration today? First, there has never been a period in Church history when so many laypersons have been put on the payroll of Catholic parishes and dioceses and become full-time employees of the Church. There are now more than 30,000 such lay employees, compared with fewer than 60,000 active priests. They are taking over many significant administrative, educational, and pastoral functions, freeing the priests for their own distinctive liturgical and sacramental roles. At the same time, many of the laypeople are learning new ways to pray and to make their own lives more deeply Catholic. Daily presence in and around the church seems almost sacramental, bringing them into the Mystery of God's Presence in the Eucharist.

Lay Catholics are looking for a new sort of spiritual guidance, a new way of learning how to live the interior life and how to draw upon the spiritual riches developed over 20 centuries of spiritual adventure and exploration. They are inspired by the example of countless saints and in the brilliant writings of many who have been named "Doctors of the Church." St. Thérèse of Lisieux, for example, may now be the most loved teacher of the new laity.

During the decades following the end of the Vatican Council in 1965, the Catholic Church in the United States lost some 30,000 priests, most often by attrition. The priests aged, and there was no one to take their places. Catholic families have become smaller, couples are more jealous about having grandchildren from the few children they have and are less interested in their children's pledging a life of celibacy. Moreover, the very rise of prestige in the lay vocation has seemed, erroneously, to have lowered the prestige of the priesthood. And laymen now play so many visible roles in the world, not least in intellectual and professional life, that clergymen—despite their unusually long years of professional study—no longer stand out in these arenas.

This relatively steady drop in the ranks of the nation's priests has been almost exactly compensated for by the steady increase in the number of laypersons performing the many, many functional tasks around active parishes. The ever-growing numbers and types of ministries—the outreach that is required these days—can now be taken care of by laypeople instead of exhausting the energies of too few priests.

In certain ways, the Church may be more active ministerially than ever. There are Hispanic ministries, interracial ministries, youth ministries, citywide sports leagues, parish finance committeeies, census committeeies, soup kitchens, volunteers for work in poorer parishes, academic tutoring, choir and concert practices, evangelization outreach, gay ministries, volunteers for helping AIDS patients, prayer circles, and sodalities for many purposes and in many different spiritual idioms. Many parishes are even "twinned" with poor parishes in the Third World, with a regular exchange of visitors, volunteers, and photographs to be posted in their mutual church lobbies around the world.

Compared with the lay life I knew when I was a young man in the 1950s and early 1960s, "June is bustin' out all over!" Today seems in many ways like a New Spring. Yet still there is an awful lot we do not know about what is happening and what is likely to happen next. In this book, we will only be able to point to a select number of new developments, initiatives, and even dilemmas. The full picture will need exploration by many other minds.

With that said, let me undertake to explain the strategy of this book. First, there is not much point in belonging to the Catholic Church, let alone taking up responsibilities for its daily institutional life, if one does not choose to live in moment-by-moment union with Christ. The whole point of becoming a Christian is to become more and more like Christ, to be one with Him in heart and mind all day long and to try to be His hands and feet and heart and head during our time on earth.

What does this mean?

Briefly, when St. Paul was knocked off his horse by a blinding light, he heard an imperious voice questioning him by name. "Saul!" he heard from a voice he did not recognize. "Saul, why do you persecute Me?" Shielding his eyes from the light, Saul did not recognize who was addressing him. How could Saul be persecuting someone he did not even know, had never met?

Then a painful memory came back to him. He did not exactly feel guilty about it—it was in accord with the law—but he had afterward found it distasteful. He remembered holding the garments of the young men who were sweaty in the excitement of locating stones and hurling them with all their might at a blasphemer, a heretic already fallen to the ground: St. Stephen, the first martyr. The young victim was trying to hold up his arm against the hail of stones that sooner or later would bring him death. He was praying.

Could it be that the apparition was speaking of the "persecution" of that renegade? The law commanded the death of such a blasphemer.

Yet the Voice in the Light seemed to be saying, "Saul, Saul, when you do this to one of the least of these, you do it unto Me," as if a new reality lay outside fleshly sight but was vivid as a palm tree shining in the sun: the Lord God lives in each human being, and they in Him. There is one mystical union bonding all humans in Christ so that if you do violence to a human being, you do it to Christ.

This new vision holds that human beings live in two worlds: the natural world and the spiritual world. In the natural world, they live on the same streets, in the same dusty towns, as their neighbors; nowadays they watch the same television shows and sports, munch on the same snacks as everybody else. But they are also living in a spiritual world that draws them ever more deeply in and illuminates for them a truer and more satisfying way to understand their brief human existence, its inner secret, its purpose, its reason for being.

We begin our study in the natural world. The first part of this book is devoted to life in the lay world: work with the poor, or the disabled, or the young, or our secular colleagues, how we can spend our time and energy and talents to work for and improve our Church. This section will profile nine living pioneers among the new laity in three important areas: education, parish life, and lay ministries. Just as the Church teaches us how to live like Christ by offering us incarnate examples, we thought it best to tell a large part of our story through the lives of these diverse and highly instructive practitioners. I can hardly wait until you meet these great people and learn of their inner voyages and their creative work in the world.

The second part of this book is devoted to life in the spiritual world. How can we learn to live in that inner world in a way that heightens our vision of the ordinary? As with everything else, it is best to be taught the fundamentals and then to learn by doing through practical exercises. We offer here just a tiny taste of a larger life to become skilled in. To become at home in.

Bill and I are indebted to our great assistants, Naomi Schaefer Riley and Elizabeth Shaw, for their help in making this project a reality. In addition, Erin Wales provided invaluable administrative assistance, and Mitchell Boersma provided important background research and help in proofreading. We hope this book gives the keen pleasure in discovery to its readers that it did to its authors.

PART I

INTO THE WORLD

CHAPTER 1

Taking Our Knowledge and Putting It to Use in the World

To live in the world as a faithful Catholic today requires strength. From every direction, there is criticism of the Church. The secular culture, and particularly the media, speaks with a surprisingly unified voice against Catholicism. Plenty of the comments are merited, but many are not. And the Church faces significant challenges going forward. But at this time in the Church's history, we believe that a volume celebrating its great traditions and practices, and looking with optimism toward the future, might be a welcome breath of fresh air.

We would like to provide lay Catholics with suggestions of how to live out their faith in the community, or, as some pastors say, "For laypeople to live out their baptismal call, they should transform the world . . ." In the first half of this book, we would like to lay out some of the seemingly countless options open to laypeople now. The needs of the Church, and therefore the opportunities for laypeople, are truly historic.

First, some background is necessary. While proportionally, Catholics have remained about a quarter of the American population for some time, by simple head count, the Church has grown significantly. Even while the birthrate among Catholics slowed during the 20th century, waves of immigration continued to keep the Church fresh and alive. The Catholic population grew by more than 8 percent every decade from 1950 to 2000.

But the Church's ability to minister to the faithful has been challenged. During the same period, every 10 years, the number of diocesan priests decreased by about 13 percent and the membership in religious orders declined about 20 percent.

What do these numbers mean for the everyday life of the Church and its flock? Among other things, they explain how it has come to be that 1 in 7 parishes in the U.S. no longer has a resident priest. More and more lay Catholics are waking up to find that their priests, when they are present, are overworked, indeed overwhelmed, by the extent of their responsibilities. Almost half of American parishes share their pastor with another parish or mission. There are also shortages of religious leaders at the 18,500 parishes, 8,500 elementary schools, 1,600 high schools, 245 colleges and universities, and 750 hospitals and health clinics owned and operated by the Church.

Historically, the leadership of these institutions has resided in the hands of the clergy. But in recent years, much of the responsibility for them has been given to laypeople. As former *New York Times* columnist Peter Steinfels reported in *A People Adrift*, the transition has been startling: "In 1965, there were no married or single men ordained to be permanent deacons and almost no laypeople employed full-time in pastoral work by the Church. In 2002, there were 13,764 permanent deacons and another 14,000 lay 'ecclesial ministers' working alongside sisters in pastoral posts."

As of the time of Steinfels's writing in 2003, there were over 30,000 lay parish ministers being paid to work more than 20 hours a week in over 60 percent of American parishes. Almost three-quarters were working full time. The shift toward lay leadership can perhaps be summed up best with this statistic: as far back as 1999, there were almost 10 times as many lay ecclesial ministers in formation (30,000) as there are candidates for the priesthood (3,400).

As this transition has occurred, so has another. Parish life has increased in scale and complexity. According to the U.S. Conference of Catholic Bishops, about 22 percent of parishes celebrate Mass in more than one language at least once a month. In their book, *American Catholics Today*, William D'Antonio, Dean Hoge, and James Davidson note that more than a quarter of U.S. Catholic parishes "are of a size equivalent to what would be considered a 'mega-church' in Protestant terminology—they have more than 1,200 registered households and more than 3,000 parishioners." Also, like the megachurches, these parishes have launched dozens of new ministries, activities for people of all ages, and many offer five or more Masses on any given weekend.

Who is going to take responsibility for all of this?

The growing involvement of laypeople in the Church is not simply a demographic necessity. It is a theological imperative. The underpinnings for this imperative come from all levels of the Church—most important, of course, from the Second Vatican Council. It is often noted that there can be a long lag time—sometimes as much as 100 years—between the end of a Church council and the actual execution of the approved strategies and tactics.

The existence and legitimacy of the role of laypeople is expressed in documents throughout the history of the Church. But it was the Second Vatican Council that laid out this role most forcefully.

In *Apostolicam Actuositatem*, the Council Fathers of Vatican II state that "our own times require of the laity . . . zeal: in fact, modern conditions demand that their own apostolate be broadened and intensified. With a constantly increasing population,

continual progress in science and technology, and closer inter-
personal relationships, the areas for the lay apostolate have been
immensely widened."

In the document, laypeople are instructed that "an apostolate of this kind does not consist only in the witness of one's way
of life; a true apostle looks for opportunities to announce Christ
by words addressed either to nonbelievers with a view to leading them to faith, or to the faithful with a view to instructing,
strengthening them and encouraging them to a more fervent
life." *Apostolicam Actuositatem* mentions not only charitable
work and other volunteering opportunities within the Church
community but also pastoral duties, including the "teaching
of Christian doctrine, certain liturgical actions and the care of
souls."

In 1988, Pope John Paul II reiterated some of these senti-
ments in *Christifideles Laici*, the post-synodal Apostolic Exhor-
tation on the Vocation and the Mission of the Lay Faithful in the
Church and the World. He noted that laypeople are sharers in
the priestly mission, for which Jesus offered himself on the cross
and continues to be offered in the celebration of the Eucharist
for the glory of God and the salvation of humanity. "The lay
faithful," said the pope, "consecrate the world itself to God."

The Second Vatican Council very clearly laid out the propo-
sition that all ministry is rooted in the baptismal call to discipleship and evangelization. All laity are called through baptism
toward the transformation of the secular world.

During the course of his tenure, John Paul II also offered
specific instruction for the leaders of the U.S. Catholic Church:
"As pastors of the people of God in America, priests . . . should
be careful to discern the charisms and strengths of the faithful who might be leaders in the community, listening to them
and through dialogue encouraging their participation and co-

responsibility. This will lead to a better distribution of tasks, and enable priests 'to dedicate themselves to what is most closely tied to the encounter with a proclamation of Jesus Christ, and thus to represent better within the community the presence of Jesus who draws his people together.'"

In recent years, the leadership of the American Church has taken up Pope John Paul II's challenge with vigor. Commemorating the 15th anniversary of the Decree on the Apostolate of the Laity, the U.S. bishops reaffirmed that "baptism and confirmation empower all believers to share in some form of ministry." The bishops recognized that the Church "faces an unprecedented situation in the contemporary world and the laypeople are at the cutting edge of these new challenges. It is they who engage directly in the task of relating Christian values and practices to complex questions, such as those of business ethics, political choice, economic security, quality of life, cultural development and family planning."

The bishops foresaw that the issue of lay involvement in Church leadership could be a difficult one but warned that the "recognition of lay rights and responsibilities should not create divisiveness between clergy and laity but should express the full range of influence of the People of God." Without the laypeople, the bishops suggested, the Church cannot live out its mission: "The Church is to be a sign of God's Kingdom in the world. The authenticity of that sign depends on all the people: laity, religious, deacons, priests and bishops. Unless we truly live as the People of God, we will not be much of a sign to ourselves or the world."

Finally, the bishops offered this humble but inspirational declaration: "We are convinced that the laity are making an indispensable contribution to the experience of the People of God and that the full import of their contribution is still in a beginning form in the post-Vatican II Church. We have spoken in order to listen. It is not our intention rigidly to define or to control, to sketch misleading dreams or to bestow false praise. We bishops wish simply to take our place and exercise our role among the People of God. We now await the next word."

Though the role of the laity is still in flux, it is clear that both the laity and the Church leadership want to make sure that certain foundations are put in place. The importance of formation for laity cannot be overestimated. If laypeople are called to occupy such vital places in the Church, then their religious education is of the utmost urgency.

In 2005, the U.S. bishops released a document titled "Co-Workers in the Vineyard of the Lord." As its title suggests, the bishops reiterate in this document the importance of clergy working alongside laypeople to accomplish God's work in the world. The bishops are aware that "the pathway to lay ecclesial ministry for any individual is as unique as that individual. No typical path exists, only a multitude of examples. Most of the paths are quite circuitous; few are direct." But no matter what path an individual takes, it is important that he engage in a serious course of formation before undertaking any sort of lay ministry.

"Effective formation methods address the whole person: emotions, imagination, will, heart, and mind. It is the whole person who ministers, so the whole person is the proper subject of formation." The bishops lay out four paths to formation—human, spiritual, intellectual, and pastoral:

- Human qualities critical to form wholesome relationships and necessary to be apt instruments of God's love and compassion
- A spirituality and practice of prayer that root them in God's Trinitarian life, grounding and animating all they do in ministry

- Adequate knowledge in theological and pastoral studies, along with the intellectual skill to use it among the people and cultures of our country
- The practical pastoral abilities called for in their particular ministry

While some of these qualities must be developed through the kinds of spiritual exercises and practices discussed in the second part of this book, others require a greater engagement with the texts of the Church and more formal instruction in the particular kinds of ministry.

In the years since the publication of these guidelines, their message has started to trickle down to the local parishes. A number of bishops and archbishops have written letters to their own parishioners to reiterate and expand on the messages of these documents.

At the same time, a number of Catholic educational institutions have begun to take up the challenge of formation. Several formal programs have been launched to meet the growing demand of laypeople who want to take on a larger role.

Loyola Marymount University in Southern California offers a master of arts in pastoral theology whose requirements include not only courses in systematic theology and Church history but also fieldwork. The University of Notre Dame has begun offering an MA program in theology that can be completed over the summers, for laypeople who are engaged in other work. People who complete it are well suited to serve in high school religious education, parish, and diocesan ministries, as well as in health care and social-work ministries.

Boston College's Weston School of Theology and Ministry offers more traditional degrees, like an MA in pastoral ministry. With the cooperation of other graduate divisions at BC, that degree can be combined with degrees in counseling, nursing, social work, and business. These sorts of integrated programs can help laypeople bridge the gap between their internal spiritual lives and their missions as lay leaders in the Church and the world.

Laypeople who are interested in pursuing these kinds of programs may, of course, look to nearby Catholic universities. But there are organizations that act as clearinghouses for this information as well. The Association of Graduate Programs in Ministry, which has almost 50 member institutions, helps educators to offer the most thorough and up-to-date models for lay ministers in training. And the National Association for Lay Ministry (NALM) is a professional organization that supports, educates, and advocates for lay ministers and promotes the development of lay ministry in the Catholic Church. National certification standards have been established for at least four positions: pastoral associates, parish life coordinators, parish catechetical leaders, and youth ministry leaders. NALM publishes the guidelines for lay certification in a variety of fields.

Individual dioceses can also offer their own courses to aid in the formation of lay ministers. Kathy Russell, who oversees the formation of lay ministers for the Archdiocese of Los Angeles, says the process is different depending on a person's background. Some have the administrative skills or the spiritual knowledge but not the communication skills or the understanding of counseling. She tries to set up potential lay ministers with a combination of courses from local seminaries, universities, and the archdiocese itself. From courses on preaching to a seminar on "inclusive communities," laypeople should be able to find much of what they need in the diocese training program.

Finding a lay vocation can be a long and sometimes complex process of discernment. But the process does not take place in a vacuum. Parishes that are looking for lay involvement must also discern where their needs lie, then engage in a dialogue with parishioners about how lay involvement can improve the community.

The Holy Family Parish in South Pasadena, California, for instance, put together a succession plan that laid out the need to look at a range of options when its pastor retired. One possibility that they wanted to explore was adding a parish life director. The parish leadership launched a national search to find someone to fill the position. Holy Family recognized that the move toward greater lay involvement, while inevitable and desirable from the perspective of the Church, must also take account of the feelings of people in the pews.

So now, to the task at hand. The first part of this book is divided into three parts, each of which represents a field in which lay participation is growing, with the encouragement of the Church. We offer a few profiles of the individuals who fill some of these positions. Though ordinary in the sense that they are typical churchgoing Catholics, these individuals have made an extraordinary contribution to the life of the Church. We hope their stories can inspire others to do the same.

CHAPTER 2

Teach Our Children
to Follow the Right Path

The first Catholic school in the United States was founded in 1783 in Philadelphia. That the institution began at about the same time and in the same place as the Republic seems in retrospect more than a coincidence. More than two centuries later, it is hard to imagine the American educational landscape without Catholic schools. Some of our most prominent political, intellectual, and cultural figures credit their rigorous Catholic education for whatever success they have achieved in life.

By the late 19th century, Catholic schools could be found from Boston to Cincinnati and New Orleans to San Francisco. But the burgeoning immigrant population meant that demand far outstripped supply. In 1884, the Third Plenary Council of Baltimore called for the construction of a Catholic school in every parish in the United States. Over the next 50 years, the system of Catholic education blossomed. Attended by children from large Catholic families, supported financially by the local parishes, and staffed by members of religious orders, these schools were educationally sound and charged almost nothing in tuition.

Decade after decade, parents knew they could turn to Catholic schooling to attend to several crucial areas of development, providing students with a spiritual, social, and academic framework that would prepare them for life. With high expectations from parents and teachers at these schools, students—even in some of the poorest areas—have high graduation rates. Catholic schools provide a safe, secure community of learning in which all students are treated with dignity. It has always been common practice in Catholic schools for students receiving scholarships not to be publicly identified as recipients. And, of course, Catholic education aids the evangelizing work of the Church.

The second half of the 20th century, though, has posed some tremendous challenges to Catholic education. First, while populations are mobile, school facilities are not. As Catholics gained more of a foothold in the middle class and began to leave the cities for the suburbs, many of their schools stayed behind. Now the Church has the particular challenge of expanding its schools in suburban areas with waiting lists while closing schools in cities where there are simply not enough paying customers.

Today, there are 2.1 million students enrolled in Catholic schools, less than half the number enrolled 50 years ago. In 2004, Catholic schools enrolled about 12 percent of American students. Today, it's only about 5 percent—despite an increase in the percentage of Americans who are Catholic.

The financial stability of schools has also changed considerably. Thanks to insurance costs and a different regulatory environment, it now costs more to run a school than it did 50 years ago. And parents have other options as well. When Catholic schools began, public schools were not universally available, and some of them did not take kindly to Catholics.

Perhaps the biggest—and certainly the most visible—change in Catholic schools has been in the staffing. In 1920, Catholic schools drew 92 percent of their staff from religious orders. Today, they draw less than 4 percent from that source, with lay teachers, administrators, and staff making up the other 96 percent. These men and women are tasked with offering the sort of rigorous education that Americans (Catholic and otherwise) have come to expect from Catholic schools. And they must pass on the values of the faith as well. In 2010, non-Catholics made up 14.5 percent of the enrollment in America's Catholic schools, which speaks not only to the quality of education received there but also to the widespread appeal of Church values. As one principal once told us, "We don't teach at this school because the kids are Catholic. We do it because we are Catholic."

But the shift to a school primarily run by laypeople has presented a unique problem for the Catholic school "business model"—that of compensation. Nuns, priests, and brothers simply did not need to be paid much of a salary by the schools. The Church provided for their basic needs. Laypeople, on the other hand, have families who rely on them for support. There is no question that in order to continue to bring laypeople into Catholic schools, the Church leadership will have to seriously consider the question of adequate compensation.

But financial incentives are only one part of the puzzle. Laypeople must be asked to think about whether they have a calling in Catholic education.

Laypeople have an opportunity now to be the torchbearers for the Catholic educational tradition, ensuring that it will be available for the next generation. There are any number of models for the kind of person who goes into Catholic education. The Church can use their help, whether it's a young man like Elias Moo, a recent graduate of the University of Notre Dame, who entered the two-year Alliance for Catholic Education (ACE) program and has been sent out to teach in an impoverished neighborhood, or someone like Mary Baier, the president of the Catholic school system in her diocese, who has spent her entire career teaching and being a principal in this setting.

The rewards of teaching in a Catholic school include the opportunity to pass on and discuss the faith with young people. But many Catholic-school teachers say they also appreciate the lack of bureaucracy that so often encumbers the effectiveness of public schools around the country. Catholic-school administrators look at each potential teacher individually, considering his or her qualifications based on their college education, rather than imposing any number of universal (but often arbitrary) standards, such as completion of a certain number of education school credits.

As a result of this flexibility, Catholic schools have also managed to attract a lot of mid- and late-career professionals who feel that they want to try something else. The accountants who become math teachers, the lawyers who become history teachers—these are part of the strength of Catholic schools. They are people who looked within themselves and decided it was time for a change. Here are their stories.

CHAPTER 3

The Child of Immigrants Gives Back

Elias Josue Moo

That Elias Josue Moo went to Catholic school for 13 years and never once heard of the University of Notre Dame may strike some as odd. But Elias grew up in a distinctive kind of Catholic enclave in Oxnard, California. His parents both came to this country from Mexico when they were 17; his father came as a farmworker and his mother came to work with her grandparents on a ranch tending to racehorses. They raised five children in their Charismatic Catholic household. They struggled to send Elias and his siblings to Catholic school and when, during his senior year, Notre Dame came knocking with a generous financial-aid package, he took the plunge. Elias had never been away from home for more than a night, let alone several months at a time in a new state. His path, in retrospect, seems almost divinely inspired.

Since graduating from Notre Dame in 2007, Elias has been working at St. Rose of Lima Catholic School in Denver. He first taught 23 fifth-graders and is now teaching eighth grade in this primarily Latino community whose median family income is $18,000 a year. Elias's degree from Notre Dame and his training through the university's ACE program have allowed him to give back in a way that he never could have imagined. His vocation has truly transformed his life.

Elias recalls growing up in a parish that had a lot of lay involvement in its day-to-day affairs. "The priests were great, and we were one of the few parishes that had two priests, but at the same time, they were very supportive of laypeople. They worked very closely with laity, and the laity were what kept the parish running."

In fact, Elias's mother was a lay preacher in the Charismatic movement. His parents pushed Elias and his siblings to get as involved in Church life as they could. His first official role was as an altar server. When he wanted to quit that position as an adolescent, his parents made him stay. While many of his peers moved away from the Church in reaction to such strictures, Elias's teenage rebellion was a rebellion within the Church. He needed to find a role that felt meaningful to him, personally.

During the confirmation program at his parish, he got interested in youth ministry. He subsequently became a youth minister and even helped teach some of the First Communion classes. "That was one of the very first things I started doing for myself. It set the groundwork for my Catholic college experience."

While Elias always felt at home at his parish, school was harder. He excelled academically, but he recalls having difficulty fitting in because of his background. "There were a lot of times where my dad would come to school straight from work, and the other kids would ask why he looked so dirty." His school was mostly middle class and white, but his family spoke Spanish at home and practiced Mexican traditions. Elias recalls having "a lot of identity issues, especially in elementary school." But he thinks that his "Catholic education, more than anything, helped me to embrace the best of both worlds."

And there was a lot of pressure on him to succeed, no matter what tensions he may have felt. "In the community I grew up in," he recalls, "you didn't hear of many Latinos graduating from high school and making it on to college." But he says that his Catholic education "instilled in me the values for success." The schools he attended "enriched" his faith and helped him develop high academic standards. His teachers told him that "anything is possible." But success constituted something very specific in the minds of Elias's teachers. "It's the idea of graduating from college and then coming back and doing something for the community," Elias remembers.

He first heard about Notre Dame at a college fair. His mother watched a video about the school, Elias recalls, and "she fell in love with it." Notre Dame was a struggle for Elias in the beginning. He was homesick. He says he felt the absence of his siblings most acutely. Elias says he comes "from a home where your family is everything, and if you're not with them, then there's a huge chunk of your life that's missing." Academically, Notre Dame was also an uphill battle.

Elias's freshman year was the first time in his life he didn't attend Mass every Sunday. He was stuck, emotionally and spiritually. But soon enough, he felt himself returning to Catholicism, "really looking for opportunities within my faith." He became a Eucharistic minister in his dorm. And he found the Center for Social Concerns. The service projects and activities at the center "opened up a whole new avenue to explore my faith," says Elias. "You can discover Christ through adoration; you can discover Christ through retreats and experiences like that. But to discover Christ through service was something very different for me."

When he went on a mission to California to evangelize migrant workers, it was a totally new religious experience: "It was just like talking to people who were just like my dad, but in a different light—through a lens of Catholic social teaching and social justice." For the next three years, Elias was involved in service on campus wherever he could find it. He participated in community organizing and tutored children in nearby school districts.

In his senior year, he applied to ACE and to Teach for America. Elias then remembers sitting down with John Staud, the director of ACE, who told him, "You know we don't want you to just be a teacher. We want you to be a Catholic teacher. We want you to teach kids math, reading, and writing. But we also want you to be someone who teaches them how to be a better follower of Christ." Elias recalls, "That sold me right away."

So in the fall of 2007, after a summer of intensive training, Elias was placed at St. Rose in Denver. "It's the greatest challenge I've ever encountered." The kids in his first class were coming from gang-infested neighborhoods, and before they were even teenagers, they already had a tough reputation they wanted to uphold.

One boy raised his hand on the first day, Elias recalls, and said, "I get detentions a lot every year, so you and I are going to have some problems." In fact, the teachers who had taught this particular class for the previous three years had all left at the end of the year. The kids were proud to think they had driven those teachers out.

Elias relied on his training in classroom management from ACE, and he took the advice of the school's principal to heart: "Don't smile with these kids until Christmas." Elias recalls that he "may have cracked a few smiles before then, but the kids knew right away that I had a plan and that this was what I was asking them to do, and if they didn't do it, there were going to be consequences." Though he says his performance the first year "was by no means perfect," he never lowered his expectations for his students. "Aim high, miss low" remains his guiding philosophy.

Elias's day at St. Rose begins at 7:30 in the morning. School starts at 8:15. He takes the kids through all their subjects. But at a school like St. Rose, the teachers don't just leave at the end of the day. During the first part of the year, Elias provides kids with an opportunity to do homework after school in his classroom. When the kids began talking about their homes, he realized that many of them didn't really have a place to study quietly. Once a week after school, he meets with the student council for an hour and a half. Then he coaches the girls' basketball team. He is regularly on campus until 9 p.m. with games and practices. This year, he is getting the chess club off the ground as well.

Faith plays an important role in the daily schedule of his class. They start the morning in prayer, they pray before lunch, and they pray before they leave at the end of the day. Elias has set up an altar in his classroom and has told the kids they can bring in pictures of loved ones they'd like to pray for. According to Elias, the kids really embraced this idea. They brought candles and images of saints and Mary. They also chose a classroom patron saint. "Our Lady of Guadalupe became the model for our classroom," says Elias, who asked the students to consider whether their behavior was reflecting her qualities and the qualities of Juan Diego, who was asked to carry her message.

"Are we being humble? Are we willing to serve? Are we willing to be the messengers of God?" Elias wants his students to know that even though others may try to put them down for coming from poor neighborhoods or for speaking Spanish or having immigrant parents, "they have the potential for greatness."

Elias teaches religion to his students every day. They talked about God when he explained the concept of infinity in math class. They talked about the conquest of the Aztecs at the hands of the Spanish missionaries during social-studies class. And Elias recalls being very impressed with the way his students asked about the morality of the conquistadors.

At the same time, Elias's own faith has been affected by his role as a teacher. In college, when he discovered all of these different opportunities that the Catholic faith offered to laypeople like himself, he felt it was "a honeymoon stage." He was completely enamored with everything about the faith. But his time at St. Rose has been the tough stuff of a long marriage. "It was very difficult to be a first-year teacher, going through all of the administrative and academic things I had to do, getting to know the curriculum and getting to know the students and their families. It was overwhelming." He remembers a lot of long nights early on. And a lot of doubts—"doubts about whether or not I was being an effective teacher, whether I was doing what I needed to do."

All his responsibilities and the demands of his job made him seek out more spiritual guidance. "I was attending Eucharist more often," he recalls of his first year. Part of that was because he was teaching his kids about it. But he also found strength and support in the sacraments.

Most important, Elias says, he has also found a community with other ACE participants. He shared an apartment with a few other guys from the ACE program, and they had prayer together once a week. It was a "highlight," says Elias. The "more reflective and meditative prayer was a great way to unwind. These opportunities really put me in my spiritual niche."

And fortunately for Elias, those spiritual comrades have remained with him. Elias once thought he would leave Catholic education after a few years to go to law school or become a community organizer. However, he decided to stay at St. Rose for a third and now a fourth year, even though the ACE program only requires a two-year commitment. His roommates have decided to remain there as well. When the school's principal asked what he wanted to do next year, Elias asked himself, "What is God calling me to do?" He has discovered a "passion for education, and, in particular, a passion for Catholic education."

It sounds inspiring, but is it sustainable? If and when Elias settles down with a family, will they accept the kind of commitment he has made to St. Rose? The Church once had a large supply of free or cheap labor—nuns and priests. Today, 96 percent of Catholic-school teachers are laypeople. Like Elias, they typically work long hours for little pay. Elias doesn't see this as a big problem though. He thinks there will always be people "willing to make some sacrifices for the greater good," and there will always be young energetic people willing to heed the call. In his assessment, ACE and programs like it will be able to address the immediate needs of Catholic schools.

But he also foresees a need for a long-term plan. St. Rose has always worried about how it will stay open from one year to the next. The school is starting to raise money for an endowment. But Elias worries that Catholic education is not enough of a priority for some. "Catholic education definitely needs to take a front seat in anything that we do. And I think that if our Catholic schools are struggling, then our Church is struggling. Catholic schools are the way we bring people into the Church."

CHAPTER 4

A Life of Service—
Not Far from Home

Mary Baier

"Saponaro, what do you think?" That's how Mary Baier (formerly Mary Saponaro) remembers the beginning of a conversation she had with her teenage girlfriends about the possibility of becoming a nun. "I said, 'I think I could do everything but obedience.'" Thirty-odd years later, Mary, who is now the acting principal and president of Paterson Catholic Regional High School in Paterson, New Jersey, and the director of all of the area's Catholic schools, has no regrets. "I don't know if I could just blindly say okay without questioning. My personality is such that I challenge."

It would be a cliché to say that Mary is one tough broad. But it wouldn't be far from the truth either. Paterson has some tough neighborhoods. The majority of Mary's students are from single-parent backgrounds, and 85 percent live at or below the poverty line. When she gave a speech on her first day, telling the students she was excited to be "a part of the Paterson Catholic family," she was met with boos and cackles from the audience. Some of the kids later told her she had no right to make such a claim, and she would have to "prove" she was a part of that family. That experience only seemed to make her more determined to succeed.

In high school, she remembers a conversation with a nun who told her, "You can't always challenge; you have to accept." Mary responded, "I accept so much of my faith, but that's because we're talking about God and the Church." "What makes you so different?" she asked the nun pointedly. Looking back, she says, "Ohhh, it got me in trouble."

It's hard to imagine how Mary, with her no-nonsense black suit and white blouse, could have gotten to where she is without the instinct to challenge. Not that she was much of a rebel, she emphasizes. Having grown up in a Catholic enclave in Bayonne, New Jersey, she looks back fondly on her childhood. "You had your home family and you had your school family." And the transition between the two was almost seamless. Her family went to church every Sunday for 9 o'clock Mass. "If you didn't go to 9 o'clock, you had to have a note for the nun the next day in school." With regard to discipline, she recalls, the parents and the teachers were always on the same page. "If you did something wrong, you went home and Mom would always say, 'What did you do wrong?' It was never 'What did that nun say to you?'" In one of her classes, there were 52 students and one teacher, and never a significant discipline problem.

Mary went to Saint Peter's College, then on to New York University for a master's degree in public policy, but she completed her graduate degree at Fairleigh Dickinson University with a concentration in educational leadership, an experience she found "eye-opening." She began to realize that there was a big world out there. "I met diversity," she remembers, laughing a little. "It was very intriguing to meet people of different faiths and cultures. And some people didn't believe in God. Some people were indifferent to God. Some people didn't have a God. But they were good people, you know?" She had heated discussions with friends from all backgrounds. Ultimately, all of this arguing and challenging led her to think she was meant to become a lawyer.

She applied to law school but didn't end up going. Instead, she met her husband. Only a few short years later, her two sons led her back to the world of Catholic education. When her eldest son, John, began kindergarten at a suburban Catholic school, she recalls that "of course, I volunteered for everything. Everything you could do at that school, I did."

Eventually, Mary took a teaching position at her sons' elementary school, an institution she came to love even more than the one she had grown up in. "It seemed warmer. It didn't seem so detached. The Franciscan charisma was so different. They're very warm, very humble. I was so taken by that. You get enveloped into a faith community."

Whatever the community gave her, she seemed to want to give back in spades. There were small things at the school, things she hoped would change, and she was getting antsy waiting for it to happen. She remembers her frustration with the "complacency" of some of her colleagues. So she started to make suggestions. The nun who was the principal at the time said to her, "Mary, if you really want to effect change, you should start thinking about a leadership role."

Being a principal never entered Mary's mind, she says, until she heard those words: *effect change*. "I was happy to be doing really well with my ministry and having a fine family." But then it hit her: "I wanted to effect change."

There was another reason that Mary said she hadn't considered a leadership position prior to that moment: "My principals up to that point had all been nuns." Until then, she had never considered the possibility of a layperson being the spiritual and educational leader of a Catholic school. Now Mary Baier exemplifies how a layperson can successfully "effect change" as the leader of a Catholic school.

She says that she knew she "wanted to be in an environment where I can be the best I can. And that's in a faith-filled environment." She participated in a leadership program run by the Archdiocese of Newark. She served 10 years on the school advisory board for the archdiocese as well. Finally, Mary shadowed a principal for six months before taking on a job as principal in a suburban area for five years, then later as a principal in Jersey City.

Her days are long and hectic, and there is always a new challenge. She is in the building long hours, making sure everything is running. She is there to greet the kids. "You're always visible and accessible to them, and you get to know them. And your faculty too. That's part of your family." Then you begin to address the problems that come up—a problem with a student, a problem with maintenance. Is there a parent waiting to see you? Then she makes calls to benefactors and to pastors and to the priests of the local parishes to keep in good contact with the community. After school, she has faculty meetings. And in the evenings, there is always an activity as well. The night before, Mary had a basketball game to attend, and the night before that, she was at the cathedral with her students singing vespers for the religious communities.

She is worried not only about personnel and community matters but also about finances. When faced with a growing budget crunch at her last school, she helped to open up a Montessori early-childhood program. It started with 15 students and had 210 by the time she left. "That program allowed the elementary school to be vibrant because the early-childhood program funded the school." That, she says, was one of the most rewarding episodes in her career.

Looking back, she realizes this was not a position she would have wanted or been able to fulfill well when she had young children at home. "You have to be careful because it can suck you right in. You could be here day and night even if you have a husband and small children." Now that her children have grown, though, she doesn't mind the hours.

The job is always pushing her in new directions. Later in the week, she was going to the First Calvary Church. She had previously arranged a meeting with a local pastor in an effort to recruit more students from the African-American churches, "and he said, 'Well, why don't you come preach?'" So she said yes. What is she planning to say? "I am going to talk about family and children first. I will quote Scripture about family and children and connect with them on that level. I am going to talk about why it's important for his congregation to think of this school as a very viable option for their kids."

It is more than a viable option. Despite the depressing statistics about the neighborhood environment, 94 percent of Paterson Catholic graduates go on to college. As much as Mary is a believer in Catholic education because of the results it produces (at a cost much lower than that of public schools, she is quick to add), it is the faith in Paterson Catholic High School that makes it distinctive and so successful.

"This is not a job; it's a ministry," she says more than once during our conversation. "You have to be passionate about your faith as well as the field of education. You have to understand mission. Because there's a need to be here. You have to understand that need. It's challenging. It's rewarding. It's about the children and doing God's work for the children."

In fact, she's often doing the work not just of God, but of parents. Many of her students live with only one parent, and some have been left with members of their extended family and no parents at all. Not having a "family unit," Mary believes, makes building a foundation for the kids even more difficult. Too often, the role falls to her teachers and administrators. "You have them for more hours than their own parents have them," Mary observes. And so it's all the more important to be in an environment that emphasizes core values. "To not be able to say to someone, 'God bless you.' 'Let's pray.' With all the destruction that goes on in the world every day, that we can't come together in prayer and face it. To be void of saying, 'Thank you, God.' 'God help us.' I mean, that's not something I could deal with."

In one way, Mary Baier ended up right back where she started—in Catholic schools. But the contrast between the schools Mary attended and the ones she leads today could not be starker. For instance, she can't even remember having a lay-person for a teacher until she was in high school. Today, Paterson Catholic has a single priest chaplain and one nun who teaches math. The rest of the faculty and administration consists of laypeople.

Back when Mary was growing up, the surrounding community shared the values of the school. Today, that's not always the case. When they walk through the doors of her school, says Mary of her students, they have safety and security and a faith-filled environment. "But we still send them back out there. And it's not a faith-filled environment. And it's not safe and it's not secure. It's survival mode when they leave our doors." A look of deep concern spreads over Mary's face as she describes what she sees as her students' "double lives."

The challenges of leading an inner-city Catholic school are not just the result of outside influences. Mary sometimes has parents and guardians in her office complaining about the way she and her teachers have handled a problem student. She recalls an incident earlier in the year in which a student was repeatedly getting in trouble. The parents' response, she says, was, "We

pay tuition, so we're entitled to tell you this is what you want."
She had several meetings with them but felt they were talking
in circles. After careful consideration and prayer, she said to
the parents, "We seem to be almost confrontational. But I want
what's right for your daughter, and you want what's right for
your daughter." So the three adults turned to the young woman
and finally got her to talk about what was behind her behavior.
Together, they found out she was being bullied and helped her
to fix the problem.

Mary reflects on the incident. "I would have just loved to
have said, 'You know what? This is just not the school for you.
I just think you need to go.' That would have been easier." In
another position, in another environment, she says, she might
have been dismissive. It's so much harder to work at these problems, "but that's what real leadership is." Now she regularly
sees those parents, and they are very friendly with Mary after
realizing what they have in common: the children.

Someone with Mary Baier's schedule, someone faced with
the kinds of problems she faces—well, it would be easy to
understand a certain kind of dismissiveness. Indeed, it could just
seem like a necessary sort of efficiency. But Mary is committed
to thinking and praying over her decisions.

"It's how we react to different situations that our leadership
is seen first and foremost. You can go either way with a situation." But that is where her Catholicism has affected her. "It's
because of your faith that you know what you need to do, in
spite of what you might want to do."

Becoming the head of an urban Catholic school has made
Mary's faith "stronger." It has made her "more understanding, more accepting, more respecting of the things in your life."
She takes less for granted now. "I am thankful for the gifts
and blessings God has given me. My family first, my faith, my
friends."

Mary is a very upbeat person, very energetic, but she can slow down to reflect too. Her journey has not always been a smooth one, she laments. After 28 years of marriage, her husband and she divorced. "I am not married anymore," she says with profound sadness. "Does it break my heart? Yes. Do I believe in marriage? Absolutely."

While many people may throw themselves into a job in order to get over the pain of emotional loss, Mary doesn't seem to be running away from anything. Her ministry, she says, has even helped her to remain faithful. She says that she can't let circumstances change her or make her more negative. "It's much harder to stand up, to be forgiving of myself and of my sons' father and to get on with life and want him to be happy. It's hard to turn the other cheek. But you need to do it." Mary readily admits that she is no saint. But she prays every day. "I pray for forgiveness, I pray for adoration, I pray for thanksgiving." And she tells me that the positions she has taken in Catholic education have helped her be a good model to her sons.

It is clear that the satisfaction she derives from her position comes from the love of her students. "The kids are so worth it. They have a lot of attitude, but they've got heart and soul."

She tells me that one of her students, a senior by the name of China, came in to talk to her one day. "I'm like a jelly bean," she told Mary, "I'm hard on the outside but gushy and mushy on the inside." Maybe China's on her way to becoming a Catholic school principal too.

POSTSCRIPT

In the months since we spoke with Mary, Patterson Catholic was closed down by the Diocese of Paterson. We shared Mary's story because we think it's still important in helping others find their vocation, but this sad development is symbolic of the crisis in Catholic education.

CHAPTER 5

Passing by Injustice— and Then Stopping to Do Something about It

Peter Flanigan

A quarter of a century ago, Peter Flanigan returned to New York City after serving as an economic policy adviser to President Richard Nixon. He recalls "living very comfortably in Westchester and working very comfortably in midtown." Getting from one to the other, however, was troubling—and not just logistically. He would travel regularly through Harlem, "a much less amenable place than it is today," and he began thinking about the "inequities and problems of the kids" growing up there.

Today, Peter is one of the great patrons of Catholic education for inner-city children in New York. He started a program called Student Sponsor Partners (SSP), which allows donors to pay for tuition at Catholic high schools for boys and girls in need and mentor them throughout their high school years. Peter's journey is one of a man born Catholic and always involved in Catholic causes—serving on the board of the Catholic University of America, for instance—but also of someone who says his faith "deepened with age." His vocation is connected to his Catholic upbringing, but his professional talents and personal connections made during his time in both government and business allowed him to be so successful in identifying and pursuing his vocation.

Peter's first attempt to fight against the inequities experienced by the children in Harlem came when he and his wife joined a fledgling program to "adopt" a sixth-grade public school class. Essentially, he agreed to pay the college tuition for any student who made it through high school and wanted to go on to higher education. According to the program's guidelines, he had to purchase an annuity up front to ensure that he would be able to cover the costs. He and the other donors assumed that they could count on about two-thirds or three-quarters of each class attending college. In the end, though, only three of the 50 students took them up on their offer and went to college. Peter says that he can't even claim this system worked for those three, since one boy left the area for high school and one asked Peter to pay for her to attend Catholic school. To say Peter was disappointed would be an understatement. He wondered what could be done.

One day after this experience, he was speaking to a priest, a young man who had been his son's roommate in college. Peter asked about the schools that were part of the priest's parish in Spanish Harlem, and the priest's response changed Peter's outlook from one of despair to one of hope. Most of the kids, the priest explained, graduate from high school and go on to college. Tuition at the time was a mere $1,500 per year. Peter remembers going to the office of his business partner next door and exclaiming, "Patrick, if you could change a kid's odds of going to college from 1 in 8," which was the college attendance rate of the average public high school students in that area, "to 7 in 8, would you do it?"

"Of course," his partner told him, and then asked how Peter suggested going about this. "Take a kid that's going to go to a zoned inner-city public school and send him to a Catholic high school for $1,500 and spend a little time with him." In the past 22 years, Peter and his fellow donors have sponsored 4,000 kids by doing just that: paying for tuition and mentoring them through high school. About 95 percent of those who participate in Student Sponsor Partners attend a four-year college, and last year's graduating class received about $12 million in college scholarships. In fall 2011, there will be 600 new kids joining the program.

Peter says that there are many nonreligious factors that contribute to the success of Catholic schools. Prominent among these is the absence of the public schools' teachers unions, which he says "are crippling the public school system." Some suggest that Catholic schools are successful because they can throw out the problem kids, an option not open to public schools, but Peter notes that Catholic schools remove only a tiny percentage of their student body—less than the percentage of students who drop out of public schools.

Of course, the religious atmosphere of Catholic schools cannot be overestimated, says Peter. "Insofar as the mission determines the attitude of the people around the schools," the Catholic mission is instrumental to the success of the students. Of the Catholic-school teachers and principals, he says, "These are people who really believe that these are God's children and that they have an inherent ability. They believe they can bring that ability out, and they work very hard to do it."

Peter calls himself a cradle Catholic, the product of a Catholic education at the Portsmouth Abbey prep school in Portsmouth, Rhode Island. His Catholic education as a young man and his continued involvement in the Church allowed him to see what he calls "the extraordinary moral injustice of condemning poor kids to a cycle of poverty in a country that's rich enough not to have that happen." Peter's anger is palpable—

and nothing short of righteous. "That those kids should be in bad schools when they need a good education more than kids with functioning families is outrageous. It's also outrageous that today, a lot of Catholic schools are closing each year because the parents can't afford the tuition—even though the tuition is only $2,500 a year."

He continues. "From a civil rights point of view, you and I know very few people whose parents didn't, one way or another, get their kids into a good school of their choice. But we deny that right to poor inner-city kids." For Peter, the proper spiritual reaction to that reality is that "we are our brother's keeper." It is the duty of Catholics and those of other faiths to remedy the situation. Peter has lived out the Catholic call for true social justice in the fullest sense we describe later in this book.

Shortly after Peter began Student Sponsor Partners, a Jewish friend of his, whom Peter describes as a "great philanthropist," asked how he was going to spread the success of SSP to the grammar-school level. Shortly thereafter, they began the Patrons Program, through which a donor can adopt a Catholic grammar school. Patrons not only help a school financially, but they also recruit a board of directors for the school and help the school's leadership think strategically about academic progress and economic survival.

Peter himself adopted a school called St. Anne's in Spanish Harlem and is enthusiastic about the program's successes. The school now has about 320 kids who are educated at an annual cost of about $3,500 per child. They receive almost no money from the archdiocese, and their test scores outshine those of the area's public schools.

But still Peter finds himself frustrated with trying to instill systemic change in New York's Catholic education system. An increasing number of Catholic schools are slated for closure as a result of low enrollments due to financial difficulties of inner-city parents, and Peter worries that the current infrastructure is not well suited to meeting these challenges. He has seen cases where a principal has been in the job too long and is no longer able to adequately address the most pressing needs: "She thinks the Holy Spirit should be sending her the kids and the archdiocese should be sending her the money." Some people will say, "Oh, we can't ask her to leave. She's lovely and she's been doing it for 30 years." But Peter doesn't think that attitude is fair to the children who need these schools.

While canon law makes the pastor the final authority for each parish school, Peter says, "There is no reason that a vocation to be a priest should necessarily include the ability to run a school." And while many pastors are great supporters of efforts to make these schools more viable, Peter says that "in some cases, the pastor is a significant obstacle." He says that "governance is very clearly a problem." Bringing in more laypeople who understand how to run a school effectively—in particular, those with success in other educational systems who can bring fresh solutions and much-needed perspective to the problem at hand—needs to be a priority.

And so a few years ago, with the help of his son, Peter started the Curran Principal Academy to train teachers who want to go into leadership positions at Catholic schools. About 95 percent of the trainees are laypeople. They do classwork for a year and then work under a master principal for about six months. The academy is recruiting its third cohort of future principals now, and each year, they have had about a dozen attendees.

The problem of poor inner-city education is not limited, of course, to New York. Peter has been active for many years in a variety of nationwide school-choice initiatives. He believes that giving poor parents the ability to choose their children's school—whether or not it is a Catholic school—should be considered a fundamental civil right.

Peter Flanigan is a humble man, and he doesn't spend a lot of time dwelling on the connection between his Catholic faith and his role in supporting Catholic schools. He clearly thinks that Catholic schools are the most effective solution to the problems facing inner-city children today. But, when pressed, he acknowledges the importance of Catholic ideals in leading him down this path. "I think the Church does teach you to love your brother. It's not the responsibility of the state to take care of your brother. You have a communal obligation."

For the past 20 years, Peter says, inner-city Catholic education has been his primary nonfamily interest. "But is it a vocation?" he wonders. He compares his role in Catholic education to the vocation of marriage. "When I married as a young man to a wonderful woman, I didn't think it was a vocation. I thought it was as natural as breathing in."

Now, having married again later in life after his first wife passed away, Peter sees things a little differently. "After you have lived it for 60 years, while [marriage] is natural, it calls for the kind of generosity of spirit on both sides to make it work."

Originally, his interest in fixing inner-city education felt just as natural as marriage, and it still does. But like any successful marriage, it is also something that requires patience and commitment. Over time, he says he has come to "fully appreciate the work that the Church does and the pressures on the Church that are stifling it." He knows that "everything that's worthwhile, you have to work at," but he has experienced "disappointments in his work as well."

Peter explains that "it's not all skittles and beer when you see things that need to get done and can't get them done." His years working on this problem instilled in him a strong sense that he must do something about this, no matter how many setbacks he faces.

Not everyone can be as financially generous as Peter, who has personally given or facilitated millions of dollars in donations to Catholic education over the years. Peter's projects have a unique capacity to draw others toward the cause of Catholic education in exponential numbers. He has made it possible for smaller-scale donors to make a significant difference in a child's life. For many professionals in the New York area, paying a couple thousand dollars in tuition for a young student and volunteering a few hours a month to mentor him or her through high school is definitely within the realm of possibility. And to think that such a small amount of money and time can make all the difference in whether or not a child has the opportunity to successfully graduate from high school and attend college.

CHAPTER 6

Parish Ministry

In his introduction to a 1990 study on parish staffing, Monsignor Philip J. Murnion, the founding director of the Office of Pastoral Research at the Archdiocese of New York, wrote that there were four dimensions in the new pattern of pastoral ministry emerging in the Church: the lay dimension, the feminine dimension, the local dimension, and the ministerial dimension. Murnion, who earned a doctorate in sociology from Columbia University and served the Church everywhere, from a Catholic school on Staten Island to a black parish in Harlem, was well ahead of the curve in recognizing this ministerial shift in the Church. Though he passed away in 2003, the trends he saw emerging 20 years ago have become even more pronounced in the decade since his passing.

The role and importance of what Murnion calls the lay dimension is in large part synonymous with what we refer to in this book as the lay vocation. It is worth reiterating the significant role lay parish ministers play throughout Catholic America: there are now nearly two lay ministers for every one priest involved in parish ministry. In 1995, there were roughly 21,500 lay ecclesial ministers. Today, that figure is more than 30,000. Lay ministers are a common and widely accepted presence in parishes across the country. But their growth is slowing, and their population is aging. This can in large part be attributed to the common conception of parish ministry as a second career or a volunteer project.

Often overlooked is the distinctly feminine dimension of this pastoral revolution—four out of five lay parish ministers are women. There are a variety of reasons for such a strong female presence within the lay leadership, perhaps none more obvious than the overwhelming desire for many Catholic women to become more involved in parish leadership in a way largely impossible during the days when pastors were the solitary leaders of every aspect within the Church community. Of course, anyone who has spent even a small amount of time within a parish knows that, contrary to the common perception of women being silenced or marginalized within Church life, "Church ladies," as they are affectionately known, are the lifeblood of parishes, and small parishes in particular. Effective organization and compassionate counseling are but two of the many talents that make women in particular well suited to take on leadership roles in ministerial services. With this in mind, it should come as no surprise that there is a reason why two of the three people we profile in the chapters that follow are women.

The third dimension of this new pattern is the local one. The personnel decisions lie primarily with the pastor of each parish. In fact, it is not uncommon for members of the parish to fill these positions. They often have been volunteering in the Church for years when a priest asks them to come on board as a paid minister of the Church. These new employees have the added benefit of already having strong relationships with the local leadership and with other members of the parish.

However, it is pretty common for parish ministers to move to a new parish. According to David DeLambo, author of *Lay Parish Ministers: A Study of Emerging Leadership,* 57 percent of lay parish ministers came to their present position with previous paid ministry experience. Of this group, four out of five had previous experience as a parish minister, either at a different parish or in a different capacity at the same parish. It is important that the Church is developing a pool of seasoned laypeople with a commitment to parish ministry and a history of serving the Church because of the obvious demographic changes discussed above.

But there are some challenges with this model of recruitment. Priests tend to hire laypeople from within their own parishes, as will be evident in the following interviews, with particular personal qualities, but they do not pay as much attention to more traditional job qualifications.

The fourth aspect of the current pastoral revolution is the ministerial dimension. In 2005, DeLambo and his colleagues surveyed lay parish ministers about the credentials required for their positions. Nearly 70 percent of the positions do not require a master's degree. Almost three-quarters require no certificate or special training.

Good "people skills," a strong prayer life, and a similar ecclesial vision to the pastor, as well as a proven ability to get the job done, all seem more important to priests when they are hiring pastoral ministers. These are all deeply important traits, but they cannot make up for a lack of training and formation. Fewer than half of lay ministers feel "very proud" of their knowledge of core subjects—including canon law, Church history, Catholic social teaching, theology, and Scripture.

Nor do many lay employees feel completely secure about their future in these positions. Nearly half of lay parish ministers believe there may come a time when, financially speaking, they will no longer be able to afford to work for the Church. About a third of ministers do not find their annual earnings adequate for their needs.

The changing dynamics of these four dimensions of pastoral ministry—lay, feminine, local, and ministerial—are important to keep in mind as we look at the new landscape of lay ministry and consider some of the opportunities for laypeople who want to become more involved.

The declining number of priests is having a profound effect on the structure of parish leadership. The "one parish, one pastor" model is waning, particularly in rural dioceses. However, the capacity for laypeople to fill in the gaps depends on both the needs of the priest and on the available talents of the laypeople. Some priests have to perform the sacraments at multiple parishes, which takes up the majority of their time and leaves them unable to spend much time counseling parishioners. Others, while able to counsel, need help with more of the administrative work involved in running a parish. And there are also cases where more help is needed with counseling. Not only can it be difficult for one person to do all of the counseling for an entire parish community, but there are also cases in which parishioners prefer a different counselor—perhaps a woman, or someone younger, or someone with a counseling degree—who can help them work through problems.

While most of the statistics we cite here are true for people who are paid and work at least 20 hours a week, that is obviously a big category. And there is a significant difference between someone who devotes 20 hours a week to the Church and someone who works there full time. In a number of cases, though, it seems that laypeople take on multiple roles, working some for the parish and some for the diocese or for another Catholic organization. Balancing these roles can be a challenge, but for the people we spoke with, it can also provide a nice variety to their vocational lives.

When parish ministry was done by laypeople on a small scale, perhaps it made sense for it to have a certain ad hoc nature. But now that it involves so many people and so many parishes, it seems useful to think about some ways of standardizing it. In 2008, Marti Jewell, the director of Emerging Models of Pastoral Leadership, and David Ramey, the president of Strategic Leadership Associates, held a national ministry summit to address the prospect of formalizing the structure of some lay positions.

Here's what they concluded: "While we had expected to identify a handful of emerging structural models and defined roles of parish leaders (i.e., mega churches, multiple parish pastors), the project found little consistency and uniformity among existing models." Spiritual concerns did not drive structure organization at all. Rather, they are driven by "the economics, geography and demographics of the local situation. A preferred ecclesiology or diocesan planning efforts did not appear as a significant factor."

Despite this apparent ambiguity in structure, Jewell and Ramey did identify a number of inspiring developments in the area. They witnessed the emergence of what they call a "total ministering community" with "a growing recognition and appreciation of a common baptismal call to discipleship." They saw lay leaders and clergy working side by side to build the "spiritual vitality of parish life."

The summit also revealed a few other emerging trends that are worth noting. For instance, there are more programs available for laypeople to engage in formation. There is more collaboration among parishes and among pastoral teams. Also, there is improvement and increased focus on Church business practices and personnel management. Jewell and her associates noted that there is now "greater accountability in parish life and transparency in personnel management, financial management and ethical standards of conduct in dealing with employees and members."

The fourth-largest religious group in America is nonpracticing Catholics. They all have their own reasons for leaving, but what will bring them back? In the document "Called and Gifted for the Third Millennium," the U.S. Conference of Catholic Bishops reflects on that very question: "Some have described being away from the Church for years, and one day crossing the threshold of a parish in search of 'something' they can't always identify. There they find Christ's love visible in worship, in the sacrament of reconciliation, in a caring community, and in service to the poor. And they are encouraged to return, again and again."

These re-encounters with the Church do not occur by chance. The Church must act. And in the Second Vatican Council, it did. As Stephen Pope noted in his book *Common Calling: The Laity and Governance of the Catholic Church*, the Council "attempted to retrieve for Catholics this theology of baptism embraced by the first Christians, and indeed for centuries thereafter. As such, Vatican II deepened our consciousness and commitment to lay participation in the mission of the Church to the world and to care for the good stewardship of the Church itself."

It is important to note that the Pontifical Council for the Laity, which assists the pope in matters related to lay ministry and other lay initiatives, was established in the wake of Vatican II at a time when seminaries and novitiates were overflowing.

Thus, the new lay ministry of the post-Vatican II era flourished, not because there was a shortage of priests, not because pastors were stretched too thin in their parishes, but because all members of the Church are responsible for its life. In an era of democratic governance, thriving civil societies, and higher professional education for more and more of the laity, it seemed a great waste not to bring these new possibilities into the active life of the Church. As Pope John Paul II commented in his address "At the Close of the Great Jubilee of the Year 2000 (*Novo Millennio Ineunte*)":

> The unity of the Church is not uniformity, but an organic blending of legitimate diversities. It is the reality of many members joined in a single body, the one Body of Christ (cf. 1 Cor 12:12). Therefore the Church of the Third Millennium will need to encourage all the baptized and confirmed to be aware of their active responsibility in the Church's life. Together with the ordained ministry, other ministries, whether formally instituted or simply recognized, can flourish for the good of the whole community, sustaining it in all its many needs: from catechesis to liturgy, from education of the young to the widest array of charitable works.

Indeed, as John Paul II's biographer George Weigel has noted:

> The real reason for enhanced lay engagement . . . is not that we're running short of priests (although that is the empirical reality of the next twenty to thirty years or so); it's because laypeople have certain vocational obligations in the Church, just as the ordained have certain irreducible roles in celebrating the sacraments, preaching, etc. In other words, the move to enhanced lay engagement is not pushing-the-panic-button; it's implementing the comprehensive vision of Vatican II.

Still, there is some tension in parishes as a result of this development, and it is useful to recognize. Some have observed more acceptance of lay ministry in the pews than among the members of the clergy. On some level, this is not surprising. Whether lay or clergy, we are all human, and when someone encroaches on our role in some way, we may object. But this is a short-term problem for the Church. In the long term, the fact that the parishioners are accepting of these developments is very encouraging.

As Archbishop Charles Chaput of Denver noted is his 2009 address "Public Life and the Lay Vocation":

> Laypeople have exactly the same dignity as clergy and
> religious—and this moment in history cries out for mature,
> intelligent, zealous, and faithful lay leaders in an urgent way.
> Priests and bishops cannot do the work of laypeople.

But most encouraging is the fact that thousands of Catholics are feeling a pull toward the Church, a call from God. They feel a movement of the Holy Spirit in their lives. As one lay minister in the Diocese of Rochester commented, "The calling comes in pieces. First, you discover your calling. Next, there is a process of discernment. Then, at some point, you get the affirmation of the Church and feedback from the community, the People of God. It is much more than just a job. There is a spiritual strength that allows me to be fed, to feed, to be fulfilled, and to fulfill."

As spiritually fulfilling as many of these positions in lay ministry can be, they are also very down to earth, close to where the rubber hits the road. The administrative functions of a parish are many, complex, and exceedingly practical. Thus, the need for new reinforcements to support the traditional liturgical roles of priests and bishops has become quite acute.

Although exact figures are impossible to obtain, it has been estimated that the Church in America employs more than a million people (the same order of magnitude as the U.S. Army, for example), with an annual operating budget of about $100 billion. To give just a snapshot, in 2006, the U.S. bishops reported that there were 18,992 parishes serving a population of more than 69 million faithful; 573 Catholic hospitals that had treated almost 85 million patients in 2005; and 6,511 elementary schools and 1,354 high schools, with just about 2.5 million students enrolled. This is not to mention a vast array of other services and facilities, from retreat centers and nursing homes to other charitable operations serving immigrants, addicts, the homeless, and countless others in need. Needless to say, all of this work done in the name of the Church requires the same operational and managerial skills necessary in the corporate world—but also a much higher degree of insight into the workings of the human soul.

Let's turn our attention now to some of the positions for laypeople in parish ministry. The pastoral associate is usually the No. 2 position in the parish. The role involves oversight of a number of parish ministries and a number of other deputy duties. For instance, they may organize prayer services, offer premarital counseling, or provide spiritual care for the sick or bereaved. They may be responsible for welcoming new members to the parish or representing the parish at community events. Their roles largely depend both on their own strengths and talents as well as the needs of the pastor. Different dioceses offer descriptions of what they are looking for in a pastoral associate. They should be "flexible and adaptable." And they have to adapt to the specific, sometimes changing needs of a parish.

The chief financial officer of a parish has become an ever more necessary position as the management of Church life has become more complicated. Because a number of people have decided to go into lay vocations as a kind of second career, there has been a higher level of professionalism in these positions.

The position of parish catechetical leader is also more often held by a layperson these days. Responsible for overseeing religious education, both for children and adults in the parish, the catechetical leader is historically a very important role. It is particularly important that the person occupying this role have a strong theological background and have undergone a serious formation process.

There are other, less time-consuming roles that laypeople may occupy as well. Though they may only require a few hours a week of work, they are deeply important as they involve oversight of the parish. For example, the role of the parish finance council is fairly self-explanatory, but it has become particularly important in an era when people have lost some of their trust in the Church's leadership.

The revised Code of Canon Law (1983) mandates that every parish have a finance council in which "the Christian faithful . . . aid the pastor in the administration of parish goods" (Canon 537). The code also mandated that "a pastoral council is to be established in each parish, over which the pastor presides and in which the Christian faithful, together with those who share in pastoral care by virtue of their office in the parish, assist in fostering pastoral activity" (Canon 536). As William V. D'Antonio wrote in *American Catholics Today: New Realities of Their Faith and Their Church,* "These and many other opportunities are opening up new avenues for lay involvement in the Church. Such involvement was unimaginable in the immigrant Church of a century ago, in which lay Catholics were expected to 'pay, pray, and obey.'"

Serving on a pastoral council can also be an invaluable service that a layperson can perform in the parish. Though the position is part time and usually temporary, the men and women who take on these roles must be serious in their commitment. According to "*Omnes Christifideles*, the Sacred Congregation for the Clergy's 1973 Private Letter on 'Pastoral Councils,'" "The pastoral council, therefore, can give the bishop great help by presenting him with proposals and suggestions—regarding missionary, catechetical and apostolic undertakings within the diocese; concerning the promotion of doctrinal formation and the sacramental life of the faithful; concerning pastoral activities to help the priests in the various social and territorial areas of the diocese; concerning public opinion on matters pertaining to the Church as it is more likely to be fostered in the present time; etc."

The document goes on to say, "The pastoral council can also be extremely useful for mutual communication of experiences and for proposed undertakings of various types by which the concrete needs of the people of the diocese may become clearer to the bishop and a more opportune means of pastoral action may be suggested to him."

The opportunities for laypeople are too numerous to describe here, but we offer a list below to give readers a taste of what is available. Whether your interests lie in music or finances, working with children or the elderly, or in more intellectual pursuits or service, there is almost certainly a role for you in the parish.

Youth Ministry
Adult Education and Formation Ministry
Baptism Ministry
Spirituality and Health Ministries
Active Duty Prayer List Ministry
Hospitality Ministry

AIDS Ministry
Stephen Ministry
Catholic Social Teaching Ministry
Campus Ministry (for middle and high schools)
Sacramental Preparation
Career Networking Ministry
Information Technology Ministry
Finance Council Ministry
Garden Ministry
Operations Director
Fair-Trade Ministry
Bereavement/Grief Support Ministries
Environmental Ministry
Religious Education Programs
Children of Alcoholics Ministry
Prayer Group Ministry
Pastoral Council
Adult Confirmation
Director of Worship

Because of the explosion in numbers of laypeople looking to become more involved in their parishes, the Church leadership has been increasingly focused on making sure that the proper training is available for these positions.

The National Certification Standards for Lay Ecclesial Ministers was established in 2006. It was produced through a collaboration of the National Association for Lay Ministry, the National Federation for Catholic Youth Ministry, and the National Conference for Catechetical Leadership in conjunction with the United States Conference of Catholic Bishops Commission on Certification and Accreditation. There are now certification standards for four positions: pastoral associate, parish life coordinator, parish catechetical leader, and youth ministry leader.

Beyond these national standards, each diocese may determine specific policies and procedures for hiring laypeople in these positions. The Archdiocese of Los Angeles specifies that candidates for pastoral associates must meet standards in the following areas: personal qualities, spirituality and spiritual formation, theological competencies, administrative competencies, pastoral competencies, and experience.

The positions described above are to be filled by individuals, but laypeople do not operate in a vacuum. The parish has to provide the appropriate context and welcoming environment for laypeople. The parish leadership must also be purposeful and thoughtful about where laypeople can best fit in.

In January 2007, members of the Holy Family Church in South Pasadena, California, received a letter from Monsignor Clement Connolly and Gardner Barker, who was then the chairman of the pastoral council. The letter began, "Wise Counsel urges us to reflect on a long-range plan for the future leadership at Holy Family. The attached volume is a gospel. It is good news. The gifts we gratefully share demand that we exercise a prudent stewardship into the future."

In response to a 2003 Synod of the Archdiocese of Los Angeles and the Pastoral Letter called "Serving Shoulder to Shoulder" from Cardinal Roger Mahony, the leadership of Holy Family began to explore how they would continue to meet the needs of their large and growing congregation while their own senior priest was moving toward retirement. "We can react to pressures outside our control," the letter said, "or, inspired by our Cardinal, we can respond to movements of the Holy Spirit from within our community and take decisive actions now that will allow us to share in claiming our future."

Holy Family began to look at a new model of governance in which the Church would be led by a parish life director (a layperson) in collaboration with a senior priest/priest minister, a business manager, and a pastoral care staff. The parish life director would act as a sort of CEO for Holy Family.

The Holy Family parish council treaded very lightly. They conducted a survey of parishioners, held town hall meetings and one-on-one interviews with parishioners, and in general solicited as much input as possible from members of the congregation. Ultimately, they determined that the parish was generally receptive to the idea, and they began to interview candidates for the position of parish life director.

The parish life director, as the letter to the Holy Family parish explained, "is a vocational minister who is appointed by the Cardinal Archbishop and entrusted with the leadership of a parish that includes a Senior Priest/Priest-Minister. The Parish Life Director has the responsibility for providing for the overall day-to-day pastoral care and administration of a parish. Sacramental ministry is reserved for the clergy by the norms of Canon Law." Cardinal Mahony made clear in "Serving Shoulder to Shoulder": "I am committed to the implementation of this form of parish leadership, which is not a stopgap measure or temporary solution to the diminishing number of priestly and religious vocations."

In the chapter that follows, we will see whom the Holy Family leadership picked to fulfill this vital role, and we will look more in depth at her responsibilities and training for this role.

Finally, we should mention the many specialized ministries in each parish. These roles are largely self-explanatory and include Ministry of Sick, Ministry of Confirmation, and Ministry of Youth. The sheer number and breadth of these ministries will strike any newcomer to the Church, especially when you consider that they are almost entirely run by the laity.

CHAPTER 7

"This Is My Perfect Job!"
Cambria Smith

Cambria Smith is a little reluctant to be caught at the supermarket wearing her gym clothes. As the recently installed parish life director at Holy Family Church in South Pasadena, she has an image to uphold. But her wardrobe may be the smallest way in which Cambria's new position has changed her life. What is the largest? Perhaps that the role—with its manifold responsibilities—has pushed her "out of relying on myself, and relying much more on God."

Cambria is something of a pioneer in the Catholic Church, one of a few hundred men and women to hold the title of parish life director or coordinator. A position created in the early 1980s as a way to deal with the shortage of priests in a number of dioceses, it has appealed to laypeople across the country who want to make use of their talents to organize, lead, and counsel their fellow Catholics.

"There's nothing like the zeal of a convert," Cambria, a small woman with a friendly face, jokes. In her office, with California sun pouring in the windows, she has the air of someone very much at home in her new position. Having grown up an Anglican, a British citizen from the island of Bermuda, she seems ever aware that her life has not followed a well-worn path. How did she end up an American in charge of the day-to-day affairs of one of the largest and wealthiest Catholic parishes in Los Angeles?

As a child, Cambria attended Sunday school and church every week. She remembers learning to recite the Our Father prayer. But, looking back, she says, "Christianity didn't take very deep root in me, because as I got older, as is the case with many young people, I definitely grew away from my faith." In fact, Cambria spent much of her young adult life wandering—literally and figuratively.

After finishing college, she moved back to England, where her family was living. She began working in different sales and marketing positions, including for the BBC. But every couple of years, she would become restless. She would give up her job, hightail it to another continent, and backpack around for a while.

She traveled down the Amazon, throughout Pakistan and Egypt, as well as all over South America. On her stints back in England, she began to help a friend, who was an Episcopal priest, with his mission work, offering her expertise on marketing and grant writing. While she approved of his organization's outreach to the poor, Cambria remembers that she felt uncomfortable with all of the evangelicals around her. "I was still in that stage of not having a great deal of respect for a lot of Christians." She says her colleagues "were all praying for me, for my conversion, which made me very uncomfortable."

Despite all this—indeed, despite herself—Cambria became a Christian. Intellectually, she was more attracted to the faith after reading *Mere Christianity* by C.S. Lewis. She also had "an epiphany." What had bothered her before about Christians was that they behaved inconsistently, and even sometimes hypocritically.

She had little tolerance for that. But then she realized, "Christianity is about Christ. It's not about Christians. And so, yes, it would be nice if Christians behaved consistently with their faith, but it's not actually a reflection on Christianity itself and what Christ came to teach us." She describes this as an important breakthrough, though looking back, it seems "painfully obvious," she acknowledges.

But her real conversion experience happened one day when she was sitting quietly in the pews of a church in South London. "There was a lovely painting of Jesus above the altar in the sanctuary," she recalls. Above it was the verse "For lo, I am with you always." Just seeing that, Cambria remembers, "I had this really profound sense of the presence of God."

And so Cambria Smith found her faith, but she still wasn't sure of her calling. Not knowing what else to do, she went off to Japan to teach English. She tried out a number of denominations during her stay there and settled on the Catholic one because she liked the liturgy. She jokes that she had to get over a few of her English prejudices before she would attend a Catholic Mass. "Henry VIII and all that, these things go back centuries."

Even so, becoming a Catholic was a long process for Cambria. She moved to Los Angeles in the 1990s to begin working for a nonprofit agency. She went to Mass for two and a half years in Japan and one year in the U.S. before becoming a Catholic. Ultimately, she said the Church "offered a more profound sense of mystery, a deeper sense of the presence of God" than she had experienced in Anglicanism. Also, she was surprised to find that even though the Church only has male priests and a male hierarchy, "it's a profoundly feminine religion." She says there is a "beautiful sense of the feminine in the rituals and practices of Catholicism that really resonates with me."

Becoming a Catholic was the beginning for Cambria, not the end. Even after her confirmation, she would go to her priest and have rich discussions with him about theology. He finally suggested that she study the subject formally. What began as "I'll just audit a couple of classes" turned into the pursuit of a master's in theology at Mount St. Mary's College. Her friends would ask her why she was bothering. Why spend the time and money if you're not planning to use the degree in your career? "This was something I just had to do, and I loved it," she told them. She couldn't explain it, but she says that "those Thursday evenings were some of the most enriching and fulfilling experiences, intellectually and spiritually, that I've ever had in my life."

At the same time, Cambria became ever more involved in her own parish in Van Nuys, California. She talked to her priest about the need for "ongoing conversion," how she wanted to help create an atmosphere and a culture in which "you don't just receive the faith and that's it." She wanted her fellow congregants to experience what she was experiencing. We should be "constantly growing in our faith and deepening it." Cambria volunteered for everything she could, she was appointed to her local regional pastoral council, and she became a member of the Justice and Peace Commission of the archdiocese.

All the while, she was running a nonprofit called the Valley Interfaith Council (VIC). VIC offered local residents three multipurpose senior centers, four adult day support centers, and Meals on Wheels throughout the area. They served nearly 6,000 people every day, according to Cambria. It was a job that she loved and found fulfilling on many levels, but her thoughts always seemed to wander back to the parish. "I began to see myself there." She knew there was only so much she could do as a volunteer. And she thought, "I'd just love to run a parish." She dreamed of getting a social justice ministry set up. She wanted more adult education, a more active youth ministry. The list went on.

And then there were the big-picture issues she was concerned about. In many parishes in Los Angeles, Cambria explains, you often have "distinct parallel congregations—a Hispanic congregation and an English-speaking congregation (with various subgroups), for example." There was "a lot of division and some bad feeling" between those congregations at her parish in Van Nuys. The Hispanic congregation had grown larger and had been offered a more desirable time for Mass, bumping the English speakers. "There was a lot of work that needed to be done to bring these groups together," she recalls. So she helped organize a number of events—including multilingual Masses and a parishwide cultural festival. Between the roasted pig provided by the Tongan community, the Indonesian dances, and the religious camaraderie, the occasion was a success.

When Cambria heard that the archdiocese was considering a model of lay leadership for some parishes, she recalls thinking, "This is my perfect job! This is what I want. This is what I think I'm called to do."

She remembers being moved by the way that the roles were presented at a meeting of the regional pastoral council. She explains, "The Second Vatican Council pointed us back to baptism, reclaiming it as the most important sacrament." It is the "universal call to priesthood, that we all have a role in the Church," that appealed to Cambria.

As excited as she was, it was still a couple of years before Cambria was convinced that this was her calling: "I needed some time for discernment." But the more she thought about it, the more she became convinced. She went in to meet with the sister who was in charge of the formation program for parish life directors to see about training for such a role. The first thing Sister Carol Quinlivan told her was, "You'll need a master's in theology." And then, as if she were just pulling a stick of gum out of her back pocket, Cambria replied, "Oh, I have one." The sister was a bit "startled," Cambria remembers, laughing about all the people who wondered why she was wasting her time on such a degree.

There was a lot of paperwork and a battery of psychological testing before she entered the formation program. And she had to take some additional classes and do more training in pastoral counseling, of course.

At the end of 2007, Cambria was asked to interview for a job at Holy Family. After much consideration and a three-year process, the parish had sought permission to consider hiring a parish life director instead of having a new priest replace Monsignor Connolly, who had pastored the parish for more than two decades. There were two factors that played a role in this decision, according to Cambria. First, Holy Family has had a long history of lay involvement in Church leadership. And second, it is a very large and complex organization: 90 ministries, a large budget, and 100 staff members, including teachers and administrators at the parish school. As it was explained to Cambria, Holy Family was looking for someone "with the skills to run an organization like this. Not only will you need to have a pretty good financial background and a personnel background but also the ability to provide pastoral and spiritual leadership."

The chance to combine the skills she had honed in her profession with the passion she had for her faith was a thrill. In her job at the Valley Interfaith Council, she says, there was a lot of "pastoral work that goes on, because we're dealing with people who are very wounded spiritually." But she had to be careful about doing "spiritual counseling" in that environment. She couldn't talk about Catholicism.

In her new role, she feels she can be "fully herself." "It's very liberating," she reports, "to be in an environment where you can be completely open about your faith."

In the two years Cambria has been doing her job, no two days have been quite the same—pastoral counseling, staffing decisions, strategic planning meetings. A couple weeks before, she wrote high school recommendations for the 60 kids from the parish who want to go to Catholic high schools. She'd been helping to coordinate the parish's Haiti relief efforts—the congregants had raised tens of thousands of dollars in just two weeks. In the next week, she would deliver a pastoral response, preside over an Ash Wednesday prayer service, and visit some of the parish's members in the hospital. She makes announcements at the seven Masses that Holy Family holds from Saturday evening through Sunday evening each week. She does fundraising pitches and writes "a lot of thank-you notes."

Breaking down her responsibilities a bit, she starts with the liturgical ones. Cambria can preside over any prayer service that is not a Mass. In the liturgical calendar, that includes Ash Wednesday and Good Friday. But she also presides at impromptu prayer services like the one on a Friday night after the Haiti earthquake. During Lent, Holy Family holds an ecumenical service and dinner, and she presides at those as well. She could do graveside services and funeral vigils as a parish life director, but at Holy Family, those are not among her responsibilities. She participates in some of the rites during Lent, offering a blessing to the elect and to the candidates fully entering into the Church at Easter. And Cambria will play a role during the Easter Vigil, offering introductions to the readings, for instance. She delivers pastoral responses that typically take her between eight and 10 hours of prayer and reflection to prepare. "I want to do the very best job for the people who have no choice but to listen to me," she says.

For someone thinking of taking on the role of parish life director, Cambria says that a strong spiritual foundation is the most important qualification. "My prayer life is definitely deeper since being here," she says. "It's challenging on so many different levels, and I often feel stretched."

But she also emphasizes the importance of strong organizational skills. She finds the job "incredibly energizing and exciting and dynamic, but there are times when it can be overwhelming. There is a lot going on." She worries that people who are not organized will find themselves "sinking" under the weight of the job in its all-encompassing nature. One day the previous week, she began with attending a finance council meeting at 7 a.m. and went straight through with a counseling session, a stewardship committee meeting, a meeting about a conflict among staff members, a meeting with the director of worship about the Easter Vigil, a school board meeting, and a pastoral council meeting that didn't end until 8:30 at night.

Because the leadership went to such lengths to prepare parishioners for Cambria's arrival, she says the congregation has largely been very welcoming. Parishioners who want counsel have the choice of speaking with one of the three priests or with Cambria. While she doesn't do any of the official pre-marital counseling, she has met with people struggling in their marriages. One young woman "whose marriage had gone badly awry" came to see her the day before Thanksgiving. "I tried to help her see things in a different light, to use faith as a lens for what was happening." Indeed, many women have started coming to her—she thinks they are more comfortable talking to another woman.

But there are plenty of men too. Particularly with the economic downturn, she has had numerous people come to her, struggling with their unemployment. "There are no quick fixes," she says, and while the parish is able to offer some financial support for people in desperate situations, she wants to help people "connect with their faith." A lot of her counseling sessions are simply "praying with people on issues causing them pain and grief." She helps them to "identify with the suffering of Jesus and help them to feel the presence of God in their lives."

Some parishioners are more skeptical of Cambria's position and her abilities. She's encountered people who meet her and "start shutting down" when they understand what her role is. They don't think a layperson should be in this role. And they definitely don't think a woman should be in this role. "You can't take it personally," she says. "Some of it has nothing to do with me. And you have to be able to see where your responsibility is. You have to do your best to heal things."

She works closely with Monsignor Connolly, and becoming a parish life director has given her a "window into the life of a priest and a great admiration for what they do." She recalls how in the course of one day, Monsignor Connolly had to perform a funeral for a young child who had died of brain cancer, and then he did a wedding. "They have to be on call to deal with any of life's great ups and downs. They're engaged with the very extreme emotions of joy and celebrations, but also sadness and loss. There's not always a lot of time to transition. They have to have an enormous amount of spiritual strength and reserve."

Cambria is 48 years old, and she is not married. But she's fairly sure she is not being called to a religious vocation. "I think my vocation is to be a 'regular layperson' doing this kind of work." She thinks it's important for Catholics to know that "you don't have to be ordained or a religious to be very involved in helping to shape and grow the faith of others. And it can be any of us . . . we're all called to be priest, prophet, and king." Sometimes she wishes she were part of a religious community— she thinks she might enjoy the camaraderie—but for now, she says, "It's just me, with the Church."

Her spiritual life and her professional life are now seamlessly connected. This can be both challenging and rewarding.

Cambria used to be preoccupied with the inconsistencies and hypocrisies of Christians. Now that she is one of the most public faces of the Church in her area, she feels a lot of pressure. "I can never be just a parishioner. I can't ever switch it off." She's gotten used to it though. "It's a fact of life. As I get to know people, they've been very welcoming and very supportive of me. I feel very loved by the community, which is a great gift for me. I love them."

CHAPTER 8

The Business of the Church
Mike Witka

In the mid-1990s, amid a rash of corporate downsizing, Mike Witka was trying to figure out what to do with the rest of his life. After working in the insurance industry for 35 years and putting three kids through college, Mike was ready for a change. He was spending a considerable amount of time each week volunteering at his parish, Our Lady of Grace in Noblesville, Indiana. When he went to a career coach at nearby Butler University, the coach gave him a battery of tests and then concluded, "You know, it is clear that your avocation should be your vocation."

Turning an avocation into a vocation is what drives many laypeople to take full- or part-time positions with the Church. They say it provides them with a kind of unity of purpose in their lives: they do not have to divide their time between the job they do to earn a living and the volunteering they do because they want to participate more fully in their faith.

Mike didn't quit his job right away. He started a distance-learning master's program at Loyola University in New Orleans in order to get a degree in pastoral studies. For four years, he participated in a group study in Indianapolis and took classes that included Old Testament, New Testament, canon law, and liturgy. His classes were held once a week, but he studied and wrote his papers every morning from 4 a.m. to 6 a.m. At the same time, he was holding a full-time job and volunteering as a soccer coach. His wife tells him that he has trouble saying no to people. And he doesn't deny it. Then again, his wife is a campus minister, and she too admits to being a little overcommitted.

Mike wasn't sure exactly where the degree in pastoral studies would lead him. Others in his class went on to be members of the permanent deaconate. But Mike already had an area of expertise—finance—that he knew could be of use to the Church.

Leaving the business world, Mike understood, would be a change. He knew that working for the Church can take a toll. He moved to Noblesville in 1980, at a time when the town and the parish were beginning to expand. As parish council president, he began a long-range planning process to look at the possibility of splitting one parish into two in order to accommodate the growing population. For five years, the parish members studied the situation from every possible angle—demographics to finances. Finally, they decided to build a bigger facility and move it to the edge of town.

"There were people who were hurt by that," Mike sighs. They told Mike and the other parish leaders that they wouldn't "need" a bigger facility. He realized early on that whenever you make a big decision, "there will always be some grumbling about that." It can be "pretty hateful," he laments. And certainly he spent a lot of his time and energy trying to get all of the sides to agree.

In the end, Mike knows the move was worth it. The parish went from having a capacity of a few hundred families to 2,000. They built an elementary school to accommodate 500 children from pre-K to eighth grade. And the staff went from about a dozen people to almost 70, including the school personnel. Still, he says, he had to be "a little bit thick-skinned. I'm trying to do this for the greater good, and I know it's not going to please everyone."

That was a valuable lesson for Mike, and it's one he carries with him now in his position as the director of business and administration at his parish and as the director of parish financial services and director of risk management for the archdiocese.

When he finished his degree at Loyola, Mike didn't necessarily intend to work at his own parish. He mentioned to his pastor, Father Jim Bates, that he would be looking for positions, and Father Bates invited him to come on board at Our Lady of Grace. "We don't want to lose you to someone else," he told Mike.

At the parish, Mike oversees the maintenance of church facilities and manages personnel. The church has two priests and plenty of laypeople in a variety of ministries. Mike says, "I don't do counseling . . . or I don't intentionally do counseling." It may not be a part of Mike's official job description, but as someone who helps decide how much financial aid they can give to families enrolled in the parish school, Mike can't help but hear about their struggles. And when he can, he offers them advice.

In fact, broadly speaking, counseling is what Mike does in his job at the archdiocese as well. He goes to the over 150 churches and schools that are under diocesan control and helps them with financial matters: deciding what kind of insurance to buy, figuring out how and what to pay the staff, what kind of facilities they need, etc. In the past couple of years, his services have been even more valuable.

During the financial boom years, he says, a lot of parishes really expanded. They experienced what Mike calls "ministry creep." "They started doing a lot of things just because someone would have an idea." But now that everyone is getting squeezed financially, Mike comes in and says, "What is the core vision for your parish?" Then he helps them build the parish around that mission. "You're not called to do 100 different things," he tells them. "If you're called to do one thing," he asks, "what is it?"

These are not easy decisions to make. Mike helps principals decide what to do when their student body shrinks and they have too many teachers on staff. He helps them with marketing the schools and figuring out how to manage enrollment expectations. There are a lot of people who work for the Church—priests, school principals, ministry leaders—who are not trained to deal with financial matters, but they are faced with them regularly. Mike is the guy they can turn to with their questions.

The demands of his job are never the same from one day to the next. He has been called in to assess damage to buildings from hurricanes and tornadoes, and even, sadly, from an arsonist. He goes out to visit the churches and talk to the leaders about the best way to get everything back together quickly and serve parishioners most effectively.

"Being in the insurance world," he recalls, "I felt like I was helping people understand a product or I was helping people understand the way their policy worked or what their exposures were." In his new role, though, "I'm dealing with people on a different level, and I feel like I'm there to help them in a different way." He got a degree in secondary education in college and thinks, "I guess that's why I wanted to be a teacher. Because I wanted to be able to help people."

And he is always on call. "There's no such thing as vacation from your vocation," he jokes.

Mike has been pleasantly surprised by the amount of autonomy he has to do his job. Though Mike describes the priest that he worked with initially as "very hands-on" and the kind of guy who "needed to know everything," he trusted Mike to get things done. The two had worked together on the building of the new parish, so they had a long relationship even before Mike started in this position. And the pastor clearly respected Mike's opinions.

Though Mike tries to bring his professional business experience to bear on his job, he recognizes that working for the Church is just different in some ways. "It's a lot slower," he notes. "Decisions take a lot longer." In fact, he estimates that business decisions that take place in the Church can take three times longer because so many people needed to be included in the process. Still, he says, "most of the dollars-and-cents business applications are pretty much the same as they would be at a large business."

At the archdiocese, Mike feels his role is a little different because he is not a priest. "When I'm going out and consulting to parishes, I don't have management control over what they're going to do. All I can do is advise." He suggests some options, but "at the end of the day, I get in my car and drive home." In dealing with members of the clergy, he says, his experiences have been mixed. "Some want to listen to you. Some really want outside help. Others just listen to you out of courtesy."

In order to develop the best possible relationships, Mike recommends that people who are interested in parish administration "should really learn the structure of the Church, really understand it." They should not "come in with guns blazing thinking you're going to change the world." After people have been in the position for a year and they have the lay of the land, then they can "make their imprint," he says.

This isn't just tactical advice from Mike. He has actually learned a lot about his job and his faith from his colleagues at the parish. "My faith grew a lot from being exposed to a lot of different people . . . I think that just being around people that are energized by their faith—that's what attracted me to wanting to do this."

Even when he is not working, Mike tries to find other laypeople who will help him on his faith journey. It's been more than 30 years since he got involved with Cursillo. Founded in the middle of the 20th century, Cursillo is a lay organization that tries to provide Christians with a more personal basis for their faith. The courses he took through Cursillo, Mike says, allowed him to really examine his spiritual life.

Mike regularly asks himself the questions that Cursillo asks: What is your prayer life like? What are you studying? What is your action and how are you treating other people? Every morning, he prays, he studies a bit of Scripture, and he writes in his journal about the ways that God entered his life the previous day. He also gets together on Fridays with a group of men in the church to talk about their week, what they've done, what they've studied, etc. Mike says that with all the chaos of his work, he needs the support group to "keep him grounded and moving forward."

CHAPTER 9

"My Credentials Are My Baptism"

Kathleen Kichline

As a child, one of Kathleen Kichline's favorite activities was "God talk." She remembers that she used to love asking her friends and family, "What do you think it was like for Jesus when he was a little boy?" The eldest of eight children and a student of Catholic schools from kindergarten through high school, Kathleen had plenty of interlocutors. But she longed for even more. One day, riding a bus, she remembers thinking that "no one would sit down next to a priest or a nun unless they wanted to have a 'God talk.'" "That would be a wonderful thing," she concluded, people always coming to chat with you about these matters. And she began to think about how she could do God talk all day long.

Now it seems that she has gotten her wish. For the past 24 years, Kathleen Kichline has been a pastoral associate at St. Thomas More parish outside Seattle.

While Kathleen hoped to do some of the work that clergy do, she knew she wanted a family. She dropped out of Connecticut College after three years to get married. She and her husband, who was in the Coast Guard, moved out to the West

Coast and had two children soon thereafter. She volunteered at her parish in various capacities while her children were growing up and even did some part-time work in a neighboring parish.

But when her kids were teenagers, Kathleen decided it was time to go back to school to finish her undergraduate degree. In 1991, she completed college and promptly enrolled at Seattle University School of Theology and Ministry to get a master's degree in pastoral studies. Meanwhile, her own parish was going through a time of downsizing. The archdiocese was only assigning one priest to St. Thomas More instead of the two they had had all along. That's when the remaining priest decided to look for a pastoral associate to help him.

Kathleen had not completed her pastoral studies degree when she took on the role. In retrospect, she thinks she was "underqualified" for the position, but the priest knew her and trusted her. He knew that theological education was going to be a weak point for her for a while. As much as she felt thrown into "the deep end of the pool," Kathleen also found the experience thrilling. "Everything I learned in school was immediately applicable," she recalls.

In the past quarter-century, Kathleen's responsibilities have changed depending on the needs of the parish, the other staff available, and her own interests. She used to oversee more of the administrative elements of the church, but now a parish administrator takes care of most of that. As much as she thinks it's useful to know about personnel matters, the physical plant, and the finances, she was "happy to let that go."

But Kathleen does oversee many of the parish's ministries. She is responsible for training the lectors and Eucharistic ministers, as well as the parishioners who are doing hospital visits. She is in charge of the liturgy commission, including the ushers and any musicians. And she does some Communion services as well.

As a layperson, Kathleen is not able to offer the sacrifice of the Mass, wherein Hosts are consecrated so that they become, through transubstantiation, the Body of Christ. But she can distribute Hosts that were so consecrated at an earlier Mass. Her role, she says, "is to be comfortable presiding and to lead people in prayer." Over the years, she has also offered some reflections on Scripture to the parishioners and has written penance services. She coordinates the services for Holy Week, assigning readings to different parishioners. And she presides over some graveside services as well.

Education is also a large part of Kathleen's role. The parish has a counselor on staff, but Kathleen meets with all of the engaged couples to talk to them about the spiritual aspects of their marriage and the meaning of marriage as a sacrament. She has developed and teaches a women's Bible study titled *Sisters in Scripture* that has since been published by Paulist Press. "It's something I get hugely excited about," she says. "It's very life-giving to me."

Finally, Kathleen is in charge of making ecumenical connections with the community. She meets with the ministers in the area to talk about ways they can cooperate in community efforts and celebrate holidays together. But she has also gone to other churches to give talks about theology. She recently led an ecumenical Bible study with her own Catholic parish and the neighboring Presbyterian and American Baptist churches.

If it sounds like Kathleen has, at one point or another, performed almost every role in her parish, that's because she has. She has worked with several priests over the years, and they have given her smaller and larger responsibilities. But there was a time in the 1990s when the priest went on leave and the diocese sent the parish a missionary priest. He only performed the sacraments, and Kathleen did everything else. She even preached every other Sunday.

"I absolutely loved it," Kathleen recalls. "I was just doing everything that needed to be done, and it was pretty amazing to me because what I discovered was that the pastoral needs of people were being met and we were doing all the things we needed to do." She does not want to suggest in any way that the priest isn't needed. "I'm just saying there is a huge amount of energy here that people just need to be empowered to use."

There are some laypeople (and some clergy) who have been surprised by the extent of Kathleen's involvement. She says that it depends on what parish they're coming from and how long it's been since they've come to church. "They don't know what a pastoral associate is, generally."

But the vast majority of parishioners are ultimately very accepting of Kathleen. "Frankly," she says, "it's so hard for people to get the priest's time. It's not because the priest isn't available," but he is overwhelmed with requests. When they find out Kathleen can help them, "they're just kind of relieved."

In recent years, Kathleen says, her role has somewhat diminished. Since the Roman Missal of 1995, she says, her role "is less public." While she is at every Mass and she makes announcements and greets the parishioners, she says, "I am not in the pulpit preaching like I was."

For the people who wonder about her authority to be engaged in the kinds of counseling and theological conversations that she is, Kathleen points them to the wall of her office. There visitors will find a framed copy of her baptismal certificate, surrounded by eight black-and-white snapshots of her family on baptism day. Her master of divinity degree is on the wall too, but Kathleen says, "My credentials are my baptism. I don't have another sacrament. I don't have ordination." She used to think about that in negative terms, but she no longer does. "If I ever exhaust the potential of my baptism, that would be one thing, but that has yet to happen. So I think I'm doing what I was initially baptized as a priest, prophet, and king to do." That is where she gets her "authorization to speak."

Kathleen has always been interested in talking about God. But her role as a pastoral associate has changed the nature of her faith significantly. "I try to receive each person who comes in the church door as having something to reveal to me of who God is." She didn't always have this attitude.

She remembers, when her children were born, "feeling so responsible for teaching them about God, for passing on and instilling the faith." But then she says she realized that "they're the ones who most recently arrived from the face of God, not me. So my posture became to learn from them. They're in a relationship with God, and it's my job to be there and have a front-row seat, to facilitate it and to learn from it."

It's that posture, Kathleen says, that she has taken into her ministry. If a young couple comes to her for premarital counseling and the man is not Catholic, for instance, Kathleen says her job is not to persuade him to join the Church; it is her role to find out what he thinks of all of this, to help the couple find out for themselves how this will work for them.

In that particular case, though, Kathleen might be able to draw on her own experience to help. Her own husband is not Catholic. She believes it is important for her to be able to draw strength from her own life and her own family when helping her fellow parishioners. It makes her brand of counseling different from that of her colleagues who are members of the clergy. "We're different from the priests, but I don't think it's less than. It's other than." As a mother, she has also been able to offer her parishioners some insights on the spiritual aspects of motherhood. She works with young mothers in a group called Ministry of Mothers Sharing, an outreach of St. Paul's Benedictine Monastery.

Having a family—and Kathleen counts not only her children and her husband but also all of her siblings and their children—

can make it more difficult to throw herself entirely into a vocation. She didn't start in this role until her children were more self-sufficient. And she could devote a large number of hours—sometimes 12 a day—to the role. Interestingly, she says that her husband has probably been more understanding of her commitment because of his background in the military. If she were to talk to someone interested in becoming a pastoral associate, she might warn them that it is not compatible with every stage of life. When her kids got to be young adults, though, Kathleen says, they didn't see her role as a job. She remembers her son saying to her that being a pastoral associate "is not what you do; it's who you are."

Aside from the tremendous commitment, Kathleen says that her biggest challenge has been "gaining all the competencies that are required when you have such a broad spectrum of responsibilities."

But there are also more abstract challenges. She worries that "in terms of lay participation, the promise has not been kept." Kathleen remembers being a child during Vatican II. "It was an incredible time," she says. "I know it sounds kind of weird, but we had a man walk on the moon and this pope who opened the doors of the Church, and Jack Kennedy was elected president." Today, though, she is concerned that certain roles are being closed off to laypeople.

But she remains optimistic. "I think there's a huge moment right now. Forty years after Jesus died, people were beginning to realize, 'I guess he's not coming back in my lifetime and what am I going to do about that?' And they decided to tell the story and write it down so that their kids would have it, and *their* kids would have it. And we ended up not with a little regional cultic faith, but we ended up with a faith for the ages. Now, my generation's challenge is to say 'Okay, what do we do with the fact that there is a potential and promise that is yet unrealized?'

I don't know what the answer is, but I know we can take the same question to bear, and hopefully the Holy Spirit will give us an answer. We may not even realize that we've got it in our hands, but we do, I believe that. I just don't know what it will look like when we're done."

CHAPTER 10

Lay Ministries

It is often said that all Catholics are part of the Body of Christ and the whole Church receives of the mission and ministry of Jesus. And every Catholic is called upon to bring about the fullness of the Kingdom of God. These ideas have led to the creation of some of the oldest and strongest Catholic institutions in the country. Many of these exist outside the structure of the parish and the diocese. The scope and reach of this larger, more informal Catholic network is inspiring. From Catholic Charities to the dozens of Catholic hospitals across the country, hundreds of institutions can offer lay Catholics the opportunities to make use of their God-given talents inside a Catholic context. At the present time, hundreds of thousands of individuals are involved in these enterprises, and millions more are served by them. The Catholic Church, through its health care network, for example, is the nation's largest group of not-for-profit hospitals. The Church is among the nation's largest social service providers, offering food, shelter, medicine, counseling, and other vital care for people in every stage of life, from cradle to grave. We offer here a few distinct examples of the kinds of experiences that are available to laypeople who want to take a more active role in the provision of these services, within a Catholic context.

Catholic Charities USA is the national office for more than 1,700 local Catholic Charities agencies and institutions in the United States. With more than 240,000 volunteers, staff, and board members, it is one of the nation's largest social service networks. Its members provide help and create hope for more than 9 million people of all faiths each year by providing food, shelter, supportive housing, clothing, financial assistance, and other forms of help.

Catholic Network of Volunteer Services, established in 1963, is a nonprofit membership organization that fosters and promotes full-time domestic and international service opportunities by providing training and resources for its more than 10,000 volunteers and lay missioners. It has 200 domestic and international volunteer and lay mission programs throughout the U.S. and in 108 other countries.

Schoenstatt Lay Movement was founded on October 18, 1914, in the Schoenstatt valley in west-central Germany by Father Joseph Kentenich to help renew the Church and society in the spirit of the Gospel. It is an international Catholic lay movement, present on every continent, that seeks to reconnect faith with daily life, especially through a deep love of Mary, the Mother of God.

American Catholic Historical Society was founded in 1884 to collect and preserve materials relating to the contributions of Catholics for the building of the United States, as well as the Catholic Church in the United States.

Catholic Death Row Ministry is a pen-pal and visitation ministry that mainly focuses on inmates on death row. The participants' mission is to take Jesus Christ into every prison and jail that they can.

Catholic League for Religious and Civil Rights, founded in 1973 by the late Father Virgil C. Blum, S.J., is the nation's largest Catholic civil rights organization. The organization defends the religious freedom and free-speech rights of Catholics—lay and clergy alike—to participate in American public life without defamation or discrimination.

Catholic Relief Services (CRS), founded in 1943 by the Catholic bishops of the United States to serve World War II survivors in Europe, has since expanded in size to reach more than 130 million people in more than 100 countries. Providing humanitarian relief and development assistance to the poor, they are the international humanitarian agency of the U.S. Catholic community.

Catholic Health Association is the largest group of nonprofit health care providers in the nation, comprising more than 600 hospitals and 1,400 long-term care and other health facilities in all 50 states. Catholic health care is a ministry of the Catholic Church continuing Jesus's mission of love and healing in the world today.

The St. Vincent Pallotti Center's main mission, to inspire and promote lay volunteer service, flows from the vision of St. Vincent Pallotti (1795–1850), who was one of the first to recognize the importance of involving the laity in responding to the needs of society alongside priests, vowed religious sisters, and brothers. The center not only recruits volunteers and provides personal religious development for them, but in collaboration with volunteer programs worldwide, the center also works to place an estimated 3,000 lay volunteers each year, then offers follow-up support services after their term of service.

National Catholic Council on Alcoholism and Related Drug Problems Inc. (NCCA) was founded in 1949 by Father Ralph Pfau, the first priest to recover from alcoholism through Alcoholics Anonymous. Its primary missions are to educate Church members on alcoholism and related drug problems and to promote appropriate treatment for all clergy, religious, and laypersons of the Catholic Church in the United States.

National Catholic Ministry to the Bereaved (NCMB), founded in 1990, offers pastoral and spiritual support to the bereaved, caregivers, agencies, congregations, dioceses, and others through education and resources. Many members of the organization are trained in bereavement ministry and can be found in 40 states, Canada, and Guam.

National Center for the Laity (NCL) was established in 1977 to promote the vision of Vatican II: that the laity *are* the Church in the modern world as they attend to their occupational, family, and neighborhood responsibilities. Today, the role of the NCL is to keep that message alive by networking with churches and schools that design programs to help Christians connect their faith and daily life; by inviting young adults to study and apply Catholic social teaching to their lives; and by sponsoring or highlighting scholarship and popular writing on the theology of work and culture.

National Evangelization Teams (NET), since its beginning in 1981 as a one-month pilot program of the St. Paul Catholic Youth Center, has trained 1,822 young adults in youth evangelization and conducted more than 25,000 retreats, inviting 1.6 million youth to embrace their faith and develop a personal relationship with Jesus Christ.

Project Children, founded nearly 30 years ago, has since given more than 17,000 Catholic and Protestant children, victims of the violence in Northern Ireland, an opportunity to benefit from a safe summer in the United States.

Women for Faith and Family is a movement promoting Catholic teachings focused especially on areas involving roles for women and families. The movement began in 1984 with six women in St. Louis and has since spread to include tens of thousands of women worldwide, who sign an eight-point statement of loyalty to the Church affirming their desire to realize their vocations and duties as Christians and as women, according to the teachings and examples of Jesus Christ.

Spiritual Life Institute of America is a group of ordinary men and women, whose primary mission is prayer, dedicated to living the contemplative life and sharing that life with others, with a particular call to respond to Christ's invitation to "come into the desert to pray."

Support Our Aging Religious (SOAR) has, since 1968, assisted Catholic congregations in the U.S. in their times of financial need—a laity-led campaign raising funds for retired sisters, brothers, and priests. With over $9 million raised, these grants have ensured the security and safety of many elderly and infirm religious and their caregivers.

International Catholic Stewardship Council, founded in 1962, promotes the idea that stewardship is not just an appeal for funds but also a way of life. It is a professional association whose work is aimed at encouraging Catholics to live their lives as Christian stewards, offering financial and volunteer support to their Church as thanks to God.

The Carroll Center for the Blind, established in 1936 by Father Thomas Carroll, has provided thousands of blind and vision-impaired individuals with opportunities to achieve independence, self-sufficiency, and self-fulfillment through diagnostic evaluation, rehabilitation programs, and skills training.

Catholics United for the Faith, a lay apostolate group with 23,000 members worldwide, was formed in 1968 to support, defend, and advance the efforts of the teaching Church in accord with the teachings of the Second Vatican Council.

Catholic Aid Association is a not-for-profit fraternal benefit society serving more than 74,000 members in Minnesota, North Dakota, South Dakota, Wisconsin, and Iowa. It focuses on providing quality life-insurance products, secure savings choices, and fraternal programs and benefits for its members.

Jesuit Volunteer Corps (JVC) is a group of young men and women who dedicate one year to work nationally or two years internationally to work full time for justice and peace. Since 1956, JVC has offered volunteers an experience to live always conscious of the poor, committed to the Church's mission of promoting justice in the service of faith.

Ignatian Lay Volunteer Corps (ILVC) matches the talents of volunteers with the social needs of our time and provides men and women age 50 and older with opportunities to serve others and to transform lives.

National Catholic Educational Association (NCEA) is the largest private professional education organization in the world, representing 200,000 Catholic educators who serve 7.6 million students in elementary and secondary schools, religious education programs, seminaries, colleges, and universities.

We have chosen to profile three individuals in the chapters that follow: Nicholas Collura, a member of the Jesuit Volunteer Corps and the director of social services at Our Lady of Guadalupe Church in San Antonio, Texas; Marcie Moran, a Catholic Family Services counselor at the Catholic Diocese of Sioux Falls, South Dakota; and Ansel Augustine, an associate director who oversees the black youth and young adult ministry for the Archdiocese of New Orleans.

Given the incredibly deep and broad series of opportunities for Catholic laypcoplc to bring their faith alive, these profiles are but a small sampling. But we hope their stories inspire readers to examine their own talents and explore where they can best be put to use in the Church.

CHAPTER 11

Surrounded by Poverty, a Soul Is Enriched

Nicholas Collura

Nicholas Collura was not a big believer in intercessory prayer. He did not really think that he could utter some words to God and another person's life would "miraculously" be made better. But recently, he's started to wonder. For the past several months, he has been working as a member of the Jesuit Volunteer Corps in San Antonio, Texas, where he runs the social service office at Our Lady of Guadalupe parish.

"There are days when I encounter people, a lot of people in a row, who are going through tough things," he reflects. On one particular morning, he remembers three people sitting in the waiting room of his office. The first person had been raped by her best friend. The second person just had both of his parents die in a car accident. When the third person came in, he remembers thinking, "Please, let this be an easy conversation." But it wasn't.

Before he started having these kinds of conversations, Nicholas remembers, "prayer for me was just a way of clearing one's own mind and refocusing on God." Now, he says, he sees "how important prayer for others is. And I really believe that somehow my holding them in prayer, if God is good, has some effect on other people's happiness."

Nicholas emphasizes that his job description does not include being a counselor. "Mainly all I do is listen, because I've never been in a situation like this and I wouldn't really know what to say." His office can only financially help about 10 people per week by giving them $50 toward their utility bills. But Nicholas does not turn away the rest of them. They talk to him.

The Jesuit Volunteer Corps is devoted to a "ministry of presence." Young people make a one-year domestic or two-year international commitment to do service and live in a community with other JVC members. They have a variety of jobs, but their lives are structured around four core values: social justice, spirituality, simplicity, and communal living. More women than men join the program, so Nicholas's housemates are seven women. They each get $80 a month in personal stipends and $100 a month that gets pooled for groceries. Participants' rent and health insurance are provided by JVC.

So how did Nicholas end up living a life of something close to poverty on the disadvantaged side of San Antonio, spending his days trying to help desperate families make sure there is food on their tables? It has been a strange journey, he says. Nicholas grew up in central Massachusetts, in a middle-class family. His father was Catholic and sometimes took Nicholas to church on Sundays. His mother was into different New Age spiritualities. But when Nicholas went to Yale, he found religion. He became involved in the pro-life and social justice movements on campus and discovered there was a lot more to Catholicism than he thought. "It was a very alive tradition with a lot of beauty to it."

During the 2004 election, he was turned off by what he thought was the politicization of religion. And he began to focus less on campus activism and more on his own personal spirituality. When Nicholas graduated in 2007, he wanted to pursue a Ph.D. in comparative literature. But first he took a year in Paris to get a master's degree in French. Though he loved being there—who wouldn't?—he started wondering whether graduate school was really the right path. "I wanted to get out of the world of abstractions. I was feeling a little oppressed by the amount of research that I was doing. I was feeling sort of lonely just working on this interminable master's thesis."

And then he started thinking that he'd never spent much time working with people. When his friends spent their extra time volunteering, "I was just always too busy or never thought of it in time."

Becoming a member of the Jesuit Volunteer Corps, Nicholas says, has been one of the best decisions of his life. In fact, the Jesuit motto of "contemplatives in action" seems to perfectly describe this young man. He jokes that on a Friday night, "my idea of a good time is to pick up a volume of Kierkegaard." He acknowledges that he "lives in a very theoretical world" and has a "very theoretical understanding of spirituality." But he says that his JVC experience has helped him to see "not that ideas are irrelevant" but that the "seemingly abstract ideas we develop about reality and the sort of people we are, every day, in the world have direct consequences for each other."

Nicholas says that he has also been drawn to see the less intellectual side of his faith. Before, he would have been very reluctant to talk to others about "just believing in God" or "praying through a problem." But now he has started to change his vocabulary somewhat. The people he has encountered working at Our Lady of Guadalupe have made him more humble and more grateful.

"On a daily basis, I hear these really difficult stories that have done so much to put my own small problems into perspective." A lot of the people he sees are single mothers. "I don't usually see a lot of men coming in, whether it's because of pride or I think more likely because they're not the ones taking care of the kids when the marriages fall apart."

One aspect of the job that Nicholas finds particularly meaningful is his exposure to people of all ages. He is a co-director for the parish's youth group. And he delivers food to the homebound members of the parish. "I visit these older people, mainly women, who can't even lift themselves very easily out of their chairs. And it makes me think a lot about the ravages of old age and whether I'll be prepared to face them." There are days when he leaves work and he wants to "sob," but at the same time, he says, "I feel better about myself and closer to humanity and I guess closer to God too." And then his intellectual side returns. "It reminds me of the Spanish philosopher Miguel de Unamuno who said, 'Only pain which is shared can sanctify us.'"

Nicholas has also realized how fortunate he is as a middle-class American. And he has begun to wonder about his financial responsibility to others. He remembers delivering a $500 Walmart gift certificate to a mother of four. It was donated by one of the other parishioners. And when Nicholas handed it to her, "it was like I'd hit her in the face, her reaction was that instantaneous. She just started crying, and it was a really powerful moment."

In truth, though, Nicholas has never been someone who spends a lot on himself. And living this life of simplicity required by JVC has not been much of a transition for him, he says. Living a kind of communal life clearly suits Nicholas. He says he feels closer to his housemates than to many of his friends back home. "Everyone is in it for the right reasons, and we've all kind of bonded over that. We come home after work and tell each other stories of our days, and it's great to have that kind of support in our work."

Nicholas might even consider this kind of communal life on a more permanent basis. While many of the people interviewed for this book have chosen a lay vocation instead of going into the priesthood, Nicholas is still trying to make up his mind. And it's conceivable that his lay vocation is a kind of stop on the way to a religious vocation.

He thinks there are two obvious hurdles he will have to face if he decides to pursue a religious vocation. The first is obedience. And he wonders whether he will be able to give himself fully to a diocese or a religious order and make himself "available to do whatever society needs." The second is celibacy—"discerning whether it's being in an exclusive loving relationship or whether it's abstaining from that that helps me as an individual to love, to grow in love, and to love as expansively as possible." For the record, Nicholas does currently have a girlfriend.

Nicholas regularly gets mistaken for a priest in his current role. He'll be talking to someone, and they'll get up to leave and say, "Gracias, Padre." He thinks it's because he has a "monklike bald spot on the back of my head." But because he is ministering to the parishioners in all these ways, it is really not all that surprising that people would assume Nicholas is a priest. Aside from the vows, Nicholas has often wondered how things would change if he were a priest.

"Is the priesthood essentially sacramental or essentially ministerial? Is it just an exalted form of public service, or is there something paradigmatically different about a priest?" As Nicholas understands it, "it's not necessarily that the priest is holier than other people, not at all," but he believes in "the traditional sense that a priest is someone who devotes themselves to the sacraments and has this role as the custodian or guardian of the sacraments."

He worries that some of that understanding of a priest's role "became less salient after the Second Vatican Council." Nicholas counts himself "a huge fan of the Council. I think that it was vitally necessary for the Church in the 20th century, and I think that mostly good things came out of it, and I am really enthusiastic about the role of laypeople in ministry." At the same time, he believes that "one of the attractions to the priesthood is the closeness to the sacraments. Not to the ministry, because anyone can, and should, minister to people. But being the keeper of sacraments, that's a really beautiful calling and one that I think you can pursue the most fully as an ordained."

So Nicholas has some big decisions ahead of him. He still feels a pull to continue his schooling, though he says is he is less attracted to a degree in literature now than to divinity school. He also might consider teaching at a Jesuit high school.

Other former JVC members joke that once you do the program, "you're ruined for life." Nicholas says he definitely has that sense. "I know that whatever I do, I want social justice to be a part of it." If he winds up teaching, he wants to do service projects with the students. If he winds up as an academic, he would consider living in an "intentional community" with other lay Catholics devoted to helping the poor.

The other day, one of the deacons at Our Lady of Guadalupe told Nicholas how much he appreciated the JVC members being there. He said he knew that many of the young people had plenty of other options, options where they would make money, for instance. But Nicholas says it has not been a sacrifice for him. "I'm becoming involved in this community, and I'm meeting people who love me and appreciate me, and I'm having the opportunity to love them and try to help them through difficult situations." Nicholas says he doesn't like the term "blessing." "It sounds kind of hokey to me, but it really is; it's a blessing."

CHAPTER 12

In Love and Death,
Helping Others Find Peace
Marcie Moran

M arcie Moran can still remember being a young girl and watching her grandfather die. Surprisingly, perhaps, she doesn't recall it as a traumatic moment. Her grandfather was at home, lucid, talking till the end and surrounded by relatives. Marcie fondly remembers the priest who came to give the last rites. She can remember her mother and father talking about Heaven. All in all, it was a "peaceful death," Marcie recalls. "And I remember thinking how wonderful that that is a way that someone can die."

In her role as a counselor at Catholic Family Services at the Diocese of Sioux Falls, South Dakota, Marcie wants to help others—both the dying and the surviving family—to achieve this kind of peace. She worries that these days, people don't grieve properly. The priest's coming to say the rosary, the service at the cemetery, the Masses that followed: those traditions are being lost, says Marcie. "People aren't taking time to go to the funeral; they aren't even having funerals. They say, 'Oh, we'll just have a party six months down the road.'"

As a young woman, she trained to be a psychiatric nurse. Marcie worked in an acute-care setting in a hospital and then taught in a nursing school before ultimately landing at Mercy Hospital in Sioux City, Iowa. She became the administrator of mental health services and, then, at age 35, went back to school to become a clinical psychologist. She wrote her dissertation on "directed grieving" and then went about establishing a grief center at the hospital. She developed a six-to-eight-week program to help people with their grieving, which aided some 600 people during her time there.

While she was working at a Catholic hospital, not all of her patients were Catholic, of course. But her grieving program had a strong spiritual element to it, she says. People who have lost a loved one find themselves confused about God's role. "God is with us through the journey, but He cannot necessarily save us from it," says Marcie. Her clients are always asking her, "If God is so good, why did He take my child?" "If God is so just, how could He do that?" Those are the most difficult questions, she says.

Marcie continued her career at the Avera McKennan Hospital in Sioux Falls, overseeing their behavioral health services program. It was there that she became acquainted with Bishop Robert Carlson (who was transferred from the diocese in 2005). He started regularly sending clients to Marcie for counseling. When she decided to retire from her job, the bishop asked her to come work for Catholic Family Services.

Though most people still think of priests as having the most significant pastoral role, the Church has long looked to laypeople with good training in psychology and counseling to help the rest of the flock. Though Marcie does not think of her vocation as being "equal to the priest," she says that she can fulfill part of that pastoral role at certain times in people's lives.

Today, Marcie has gone back to her first love, one-on-one counseling. Her clients run the gamut, from a woman whose husband is a gambling addict to a young man trying to get over the death of his sister who was killed in a car accident. In her previous roles, she often saw people who had serious mental illnesses or maladjustments. In her current position, though, she sees "people who are off the track of life, who are borderline depressives, people with anxiety and panic attacks." The people who come to her find that "life is hard and relationships are painful." She sees people "going into marriages and divorces without direction." She wants to help people get back on track. "It can happen to all normal people," Marcie says, "but it's how we figure it out, how we work ourselves out of that," that counts.

Half of Marcie's caseload these days is marriage counseling. She works with a priest to hold marriage-preparation classes. And she is a speaker on several evenings for the couples who are engaged. Marcie has been married for 50 years now, and she says she feels very comfortable laying down the law for these (mostly) young people. "I tell them, 'This is serious business!' I give them a lot of important tips on how the things you do now as a couple are going to lead to problems when you're married." Starting with name-calling.

Marcie says that she has seen and heard husbands and wives insult each other, and "it's a poor foundation for a marriage of respect and trust and love. We have to take a look at our behavior with each other and maintain a respectful mood from day one, or you won't have a marriage that's lasting."

When Marcie talks about marriage to the class of engaged couples, she reflects on her own relationship with her husband. "I talk about how you reach a point where you have such trust and you're so good at communicating that you just need to look at each other and you know what the other person is thinking."

Marcie has written out 10 principles for a happy marriage that she shares with the couples. They're not necessarily religious principles as much as ideas about how to make a marriage work—how husbands and wives should behave toward one another. Marriage, she tells them, "is sacred and above everything else." She warns the young men and women not to confide problems of the marriage to best friends or parents or in-laws. "You take it to your spouse."

Marcie also does some work for the diocesan marriage tribunal, which is the group that grants annulments. She is occasionally asked to see if a person should be granted an annulment, if the person seemed too immature to enter into the marriage in the first place. Perhaps, more important, Marcie is asked to see whether the person is now up to the task again, that is, whether they should be allowed to marry in the Church a second time. She has on more than one occasion said no. "If you're at an impasse now," Marcie says of some couples, "six months after you're married, it's going to be war."

In her current role, Marcie also sees some members of the clergy. Some are referred to her by the bishop. Others come on their own, relieved, no doubt, that they can discuss their own problems instead of listening to other people's problems for a while.

Marcie works four days a week, but the days she works are long. She does a full day of counseling, both in person and over the phone, then often holds educational programs in the evening. She offers an annual calendar of six-week grieving programs that help people with all kinds of losses.

One of the nice parts about working at the diocesan office, though, is that if she does have some free time, she can attend a noon Mass or a bishop's coffee, for example. Her current position, Marcie says, has "given me an enrichment in my own spirituality more so than I think I ever took time for."

Marcie had always been a very strong Catholic, working hard in her parish, raising her own children in the Church, praying every day. But it is her profession that has been among the deepest expressions of her faith, she says. "I feel that my work in what I do for other people or with other people is more spiritual than anything else I could do."

"Sometimes, when you're born and raised a Catholic," Marcie reflects, "you don't even think about it." But being in the diocesan environment "has enriched my work and my faith." She says, "I'm very, very comfortable talking to clients about their spiritual selves." Some of them don't always understand what she is suggesting. "They look at me blankly, and I know they haven't thought along religious lines in a long time, but the next time they come back, they've given it some more thought." Marcie says she recently had a client who went into a Christian bookstore after their last counseling session. "I don't think he was ever a religious person, and I don't think he participates in a religion now, but it got him thinking that there is something more than just how he's viewing life right now."

When she went to school for clinical psychology, Marcie recalls that everything she learned was based on scientific evidence. "There was no mention of anything spiritual." Since then, she says, religious faith "has become more widely integrated into my profession." The "holistic view of the person" that she remembers from her days training as a nurse is more embedded now in what psychologists do, and certainly in her work for the Church.

Working in the Church has also allowed her a certain amount of freedom in talking about faith and talking about her own experience. She feels called to work with "people who are in grief, people who feel hopeless about God, who are trying to reach out to God, but they don't know how." Being able to share her own spirituality with those people has clearly been very important for Marcie.

But the most rewarding part of the job, she maintains, is getting to "see people recover." After decades in the profession, she still marvels that "you can actually teach people how to make these necessary readjustments in their lives."

As for the marital counseling, she says she enjoys getting people to remember why it is that they first fell in love. "What did you love about her that you wanted to marry her? Where is that now?" She is continually reminding young people that "marriage is a contract, that it's a very holy, respectful contract." Though matrimony can be a lovely idea, Marcie is a pragmatist. "You really have to look at the here and now and help them with the best decision possible."

CHAPTER 13

After the Waters Recede: Leading the Next Generation to Shore

Ansel Augustine

"Somewhere between 85 and 90 percent of youth ministry happens before or after the meeting," says Ansel Augustine. "That's when a young person breaks down and is opening up to you about what happened in the meeting or is nervous about what's going to happen. And they'll come talk to you." Ansel is the associate director and black youth ministry coordinator for the Archdiocese of New Orleans. That's why he makes sure he's always available to talk to kids after meetings and events, to stop off with them to get a bite to eat after school. "We forget as adults what it's like to be a young person, trying to find our place in life." The Church, he says, "is set up for adults and works around adults' schedules." Ansel, who is 33, says his job in the youth ministry office "is to make sure a young person can walk in and feel welcome and know that this is their Church too."

It is hard to think of someone better suited to the job than Ansel Augustine, who has felt both the warm embrace of his faith and, at times, the cold shoulder of the world and even sometimes of the Church. He grew up in the Lafitte Projects in New Orleans, which he calls a "close-knit community" but one that was also ravaged by drugs during the 1990s. "Violence became an everyday way of life," he recalls.

He grew up with an aunt, and his siblings were scattered around the area. His aunt cared for him all the time. She took him to church with her each week at St. Peter Claver, he recalls. But he doesn't remember being particularly interested in his faith.

Ansel finished high school out of state because of the increasing violence in his neighborhood. After high school, he returned to New Orleans, where he attended Loyola University. He was very active at Loyola and won numerous awards while he was at the Jesuit school. He loved the friends he made at Loyola, but he would always make sure he came home to visit his aunt and his friends from Tremé during vacations and any time he had off.

Then tragedy struck during his sophomore year. Ansel's closest friend from home, a young man named Pierre, was shot. Ansel rushed to the hospital when he heard, but he was too late. To this day, he still doesn't know what happened. But things at school grew more difficult for him after Pierre's death. "I was just lost," he says. "My grades started slumping." Over the summer, Ansel did odd jobs to pay for school, but the rest of the time, he would just sleep. And all this time, no one at school had any idea what he was going through.

Before Pierre's death, Ansel was an avid participant in campus activities. He belonged to a fraternity and served on a variety of committees and councils, participating in community-service programs. He would go downtown with other students and bring sandwiches to the homeless people in the parks. Informally, he started to serve as a mentor to some of the younger kids from his neighborhood.

But he wasn't very involved in religious life on campus—that is, until he met the Reverend Lois Dejean. A gospel singer and activist who served as a campus minister at the time, Dejean kept asking Ansel what he was "doing for God." He recalls, "It was really frustrating because I could never give her an answer."

One day, Dejean invited Ansel to the Hour of Power, a gospel service on campus. It began with a series of praise songs, followed by a speaker and then prayer. Ansel remembers he was put off by it at first. "I wasn't into the faith enough. I was still questioning God." But finally, the words of one of the preachers there spoke to him. A man who had once belonged to Ansel's fraternity "talked about being lost and how God is sometimes trying to put us in situations where we don't have any control over our own lives because He wants to show He has control over our lives."

Looking back, Ansel recalls, "that's when I really started paying heed to what was really going on." He began attending prayer services more regularly, listening to what the speakers were saying about Scripture and then going home and studying them. Toward the end of Ansel's junior year, he began to wonder what he was going to do next. Again, Reverend Dejean began to push him: "How is your church life?" Ansel still wasn't attending Mass regularly—he found it to be more of a "chore" than anything else.

Dejean encouraged him to look again at St. Peter Claver, the church in his old neighborhood, the one he used to attend with his aunt. That is when he started making the connection between faith and service. A lot of the kids from his home parish were attending the community-service events he was leading.

During his senior year, Ansel happened upon two brochures— one for a certificate in youth ministry from the Institute for Black Catholic Studies at Xavier University in New Orleans and the other for a master's program in pastoral studies at Loyola. In retrospect, the two programs were exactly what he needed to continue on his spiritual and career paths.

He recalls being the youngest person in both programs by at least a decade and sometimes feeling a little out of place. Ansel loved being at Loyola's Institute for Ministry. He enjoyed the knowledge that was shared and the professors who taught the classes. But not everything was great at Loyola. He had the sense that a number of the other students, both among the clergy and laypeople, thought he didn't belong. They wouldn't talk to him during the breaks between classes. "Man, this is a ministry program?" he remembers thinking. In retrospect, he thinks that some members of the Church's establishment "don't want to let go of what they think is theirs. But it's not theirs. It's Christ's."

One of the reasons that he felt more comfortable at Xavier is that most of the participants in the program were black. Ansel grew up in a black Catholic parish, but once he got to Loyola, things were different. He was out of his element in the mostly white environment. The Institute for Black Catholic Studies at Xavier, he says, is "so important to me because it put everything in perspective and let me know that yes, this is my Church, yes, a lot of the rituals relate to African-American spirituality as well. Even though you don't see a lot of people the same color as us, it is still our Church."

Just as Ansel was growing stronger in his faith and surer that his calling lay in mentoring young people in the Church, tragedy struck again, this time on a much larger scale. He originally thought he would wait out Hurricane Katrina and just stay put at his house in New Orleans. But on the Sunday morning before the storm, his best friend pulled up in front of his house and suggested they evacuate to Tallahassee. Augustine called his girlfriend, Chanté, but couldn't reach her. A cousin of hers said she had already left town. So Ansel and his buddy hit the road.

In Florida that Tuesday morning, Ansel heard that the levees in New Orleans broke. He and his friend volunteered for the Red Cross in Orlando, hoping they'd be sent back to their devastated city, but no one was going back in yet. They stayed in Orlando for a few days to help out with the evacuees. Then Ansel got on a bus to Houston, where he began searching through the chaos of the Astrodome for his friends and his "Church family."

Eventually, he made his way back to New Orleans, volunteering with Catholic Charities. He would help gut homes all day and then sleep in his van at night. He couldn't afford to rent one of the few apartments that were available. But the worst was yet to come. Shortly after returning, he was called to the morgue to identify the body of Chanté. It turned out that she hadn't left. Ansel lost other family and friends—18 total—in the storm as well.

He was devastated, but this time, as he describes it, he was not lost. He had his faith to turn to. A few weeks after the storm, he returned to St. Peter Claver. With 6 feet of water in the church, Ansel and one of his fraternity brothers hardly knew where to begin. The church, which dates back to the 1850s, was a wreck. "It looked like someone played marbles with the pews. Everything was picked up and thrown around. There was black soot or mud everywhere." They began to gut the church, trying to get everything out. Ansel remembers standing on a ladder in the middle of the church, trying to take a banner off of one of the columns. "I just broke down and cried. That was the first time I cried. I was trying to make sense of what I was doing. I missed my family and I missed Chanté. But everything that was going on, I knew had a bigger purpose than I could understand. And I just had to trust that plan."

So he focused on rebuilding St. Peter Claver. "That's where my heart was." Ansel says he just wanted to be a model for other young adults. He wanted people to look at him and learn: "If you keep the faith, God will do great things with you too. Maybe not as far as the world's standards. You might not get money and houses, but you have a lot waiting for you in the kingdom afterwards."

Ansel finished his training at Xavier in summer 2003. The program had been temporarily relocated to the University of Notre Dame following Katrina. So it was during the summer of 2006 that Ansel taught at the Institute for Black Catholic Studies in Indiana and then returned to St. Peter Claver, where he resumed his position of director of youth ministry.

While there, he planned events and retreats and did a lot of counseling. He also continued to locate church families that were scattered throughout the country and helped others return to New Orleans. During the six years he worked at that job, there were a lot of challenges—and many from parents' logistical concerns. Ansel spent a lot of time reassuring adults in his job as youth minister. St. Peter Claver's youth ministry was a rock in the community, especially after Katrina. With so many schools and community centers closed, it was one of the few places young people could still go.

Ansel also worked to get his parish noticed. Particularly after Katrina, when several of the black churches had to close, St. Peter Claver's was one of the most resilient and popular churches in the city. It also ranked third in the amount of money it was giving to the archdiocese, despite the high percentage of congregants living below the poverty line. Ansel made sure that even though the young people in his care were not from financially affluent families, they got to attend all of the diocesan events. He'd send the kids to the annual World Youth Day rally. But, he said, his group often didn't feel welcome. "The music, the speakers, the environment, they just didn't relate to us."

Ansel also pushed the kids from St. Peter Claver's to join the diocesan sports league. Again, there were tensions, but he wanted to make sure that the youth in his parish had as many opportunities as they could.

Though Ansel might not have realized it at the time, the archdiocese took note of his efforts. After rebuilding his parish, Ansel was asked to oversee the black youth and young adult ministry for the whole archdiocese and to help other black churches rebuild. He was recently promoted to associate director of the CYO Youth & Young Adult Ministry Office for the archdiocese. Now he spends a lot of his time training other ministers.

On a typical day, he has meetings and conference calls to coordinate events for several hours. He talks to youth ministers around the city and to many volunteers. He gets a lot of calls from parents and kids with regard to meetings or deadlines. Usually, he has an evening meeting around 6 or 7 p.m. and then tries to get home by 9 to get some sleep before starting the whole process over again.

He just oversaw the third youth and young adult revival for the archdiocese. There were more than 600 people from around the city. The church where it was held was overflowing. He also helped organize and emceed the National Catholic Conference on Youth Ministry (NCCYM). About 2,600 youth ministers from around the country attended this event in New Orleans in December 2010. While Ansel is less involved in the day-to-day workings of individual parishes now, he has a leadership board made up of young people from the different parishes: "They keep me fresh with ideas." He also likes that it starts the process of empowering young people in the Church.

In the past few years, some of the kids in his charge have told Ansel they want to be youth ministers when they grow up. "Man, just hearing that makes me smile inside and out." He knows, of course, that some of them may choose that path, but plenty will not. "Just the fact that what I did mattered enough to them" makes it worth it. He hopes they will not be just like him but "be like the person Christ has me be."

Ansel warns that going into Church ministry, especially youth ministry, can be a sacrifice. You will see people around you following avenues to financial prosperity. Youth ministry is not among them. And, of course, the hours are really when the kids need you, which could be anytime.

Though it's possible to be a youth minister with less training than Ansel has—a master's degree is not a requirement—he advises others interested in this vocation to get as much education in it as possible. "Our young people deserve the best," he tells the ministers under him. "You should absorb all the knowledge you can, because it makes you a better minister." But this vocation is also a communal one, Ansel emphasizes. "Know that it's not an easy road but there are others doing it. Find a community of people, a group of youth ministers doing the same work you're doing." Being alone in this work, Ansel says, can lead people to think that "it's all about you." But it's not. "It's about what Christ does through you."

PART II

THE SEARCH
WITHIN

CHAPTER 14

The Soul of Laypeople

"[It is fruitful] both on the part of priests as well as of religious and lay people to understand even better what this Church is, the People of God in the Body of Christ. At the same time, it is necessary to improve pastoral structures in such a way that the co-responsibility of all the People of God in their entirety is gradually promoted, and with respect for vocations and for the respective roles of the consecrated and of lay people. This demands a change in mindset, particularly concerning lay people. They must no longer be viewed as 'collaborators' of the clergy but truly recognized as 'co-responsible,' for the Church's being and action, thereby fostering the consolidation of a mature and committed laity."
—POPE BENEDICT XVI, "CHURCH MEMBERSHIP
AND PASTORAL CO-RESPONSIBILITY"

"Is it fanciful to think that the people-called-together could rediscover the dynamic newness of their faith in their dispersed condition? Members of the Church's great lay organizations around the world do not think so. Even as mobility

has sapped the vitality of many parishes, there has been a great upsurge—mostly outside the U.S. thus far—of lay associations, formation programs, and ecclesial movements. These groups, so varied in their charisms, so rich in storytellers, are providing a way for Catholics to stay in touch with each other and with their tradition."

—MARY ANN GLENDON,
"THE HOUR OF THE LAITY"

Thanks in part to all of the work now assigned to laypeople in the Church—the work described in the preceding chapters—a new type of spiritual life is steadily growing up. More and more laypersons who work professionally in the Church (as well as the volunteers shouldering a greater and greater burden) feel the need to shape their own lives in a new way, matched to their own different needs and adjusted to the new base of knowledge about the world in which they begin.

In a far wider ring still, millions of Catholics are feeling impulses of the Holy Spirit new to them. They sense, in their smaller or greater success in this world, that "there has to be something better than this." They thirst for eternal water, for a tongue of fire in the heart, for a quiet, sweet taste of truth that comes unsullied from the font of all Truth. They want the truth about themselves.

They want to love their neighbors better, the poor much better. They see around them so much pain, enervation, weariness, dryness of heart, sheer boredom, and emptiness. They confront a spiritual desert all around them, under the merry-go-round of the luxuriant shopping malls—and they feel that desert advancing in their own souls. They long for deeper, truer inner life. Somehow, they long for the infinite. They long for boundless love. Ours is the time of the restless heart, the very restless heart.

While these newly empowered lay Catholics owe much to, and try to deepen themselves in classical forms of, Catholic spiritual life, developed over the centuries, they still seek a distinctive way to God. Their lives are not like those of the clergy in many important dimensions.

Many such persons, to be sure, have tasted good hours of prayer and perhaps a weekend retreat. They have sometimes been awakened by a penetrating, moving sermon that spoke directly to their hearts and stirred something deep within them. In the nine exemplars we have profiled in Part I of this book, you have read several moving testimonies to this effect.

Many of these hungry ones have been deeply touched by the popular forms of inner life taught to laypeople by St. Ignatius Loyola (1491–1556) in his *Spiritual Exercises*, by St. Francis de Sales (1567–1622) in his *Introduction to the Devout Life*, and by St. Thérèse of Lisieux (1873–1897) in her autobiographical *Story of a Soul*.

But what more and more feel keenly is that they do not yet have in their hands a guide into the deserts and mountains of the spiritual life, written for the demands of lay life that are encountered by hungry souls in the turmoil of an affluent urban life. In school, they learned very little about the treasury of spiritual wisdom preserved and steadily added to by the Church. When they finally discover these, later in life than they should have, they drink profitably from these books and lessons of the past. Many feel betrayed by the shallowness of the Catholic education they experienced in their youth after Vatican Council II.

Now it becomes clearer and clearer to them that the spiritual lives of laypeople diverge sharply from those of priests or religious in three key respects. The easy one to deal with first is the stunning difference in the education and professional experience of today's laypersons and most priests and religious.

Laypersons and clergy have been preparing themselves for very different forms of life. They know different things, experience to some extent different worlds. The vocation of the layperson is not to become a "little clergyman" but "to preach the Gospel to all nations." It is evangelization in the whole world.

It is as if lay eyes and priestly eyes are focused in different directions and as if laypersons and priests have considerably different roles and concerns in the life of the Body of Christ. As Mary Ann Glendon writes:

> It is only common sense that most of us lay people are best
> equipped to fulfill our vocations primarily in the places
> where we live and work. It is because we are present in all
> the secular occupations that the Vatican II fathers empha-
> sized our "special task" to take a more active part, according
> to our talents and knowledge, in the explanation and defense
> of Christian principles and in the application of them to the
> problems of our times.

Effective argument today often requires a lay touch and lay expertise.

The new spiritual life for the laity also needs to prepare them better to live out there on the front lines of the war for souls, usually alone, not organized into platoons with a command structure and lacking well-thought-out "best practices." Laypeople regularly leave the shelter of their Church and community, encountering and sometimes doing battle with the secular world. More even than soldiers going into battle in faraway places, laypersons know they are often alone. They hunger, they thirst, they seek practical light—and fire also for their souls. As Glendon writes:

What if the scattered Catholic faithful were to remember and embrace the heritage that is rightly theirs? What if they were to rediscover the newness of their faith and its power to judge the prevailing culture? What an awakening that would be for the sleeping giant! As John Paul II likes to tell young people: "If you are what you should be—that is if you live Christianity without compromise—you will set the world ablaze!"

CHAPTER 15

First Comes Love—
God's for Us

"Nothing is sweeter than love, nothing stronger or higher or wider; nothing is more pleasant, nothing fuller, and nothing better in heaven or on earth, for love is born of God and cannot rest except in God."

—THOMAS À KEMPIS,
THE IMITATION OF CHRIST

"Charity gave me the key to my vocation . . . I understood . . . that the Church has a heart—and a heart on fire with love."

—ST. THÉRÈSE OF LISIEUX

The starting point of the lay vocation begins in the inner life of God, in *caritas*. That is the name of the immense fire of love that the Father bears for the Son and that the Father and Son together generate so powerfully that it constitutes the Holy Spirit. This fiery Spirit infuses caritas into our own poor hearts as a pure, unwarranted gift.

The Christian God is not Pure Intelligence—solitary, icy, and aloof. Rather, the revelation unveiled by Christ is that our God is a communion of persons, more like our own human communities of love. "Where there is caritas and amor, there God is," goes the old and beautiful hymn. The most divine thing in the life of each of us is the love we have actually participated in, our communion with dearest others. The God of the Trinity is more a matter of shared love among persons than a solitary person.

The next astonishing feature of love is its inner drive to diffuse itself to others. St. Thérèse grasped this point so well, as she wrote, "Love is all things . . . love is eternal, reaching down through the ages and stretching to the uttermost limits of earth." One of Michael's daughters was once extremely lonely at school overseas, so much so that he began arranging a lecture at her university so he could fly out to see her. He was very worried, and so was his wife.

Three weeks later, Michael was again talking to his daughter, and this time, she was buoyant, happy, and overflowing. He found himself asking her over the phone, "Have you met a guy?" She was silent just a moment, then said, "How did you know?"

Love cannot help revealing itself.

Christian love has a special sign. If a person says he loves God but does not love those around him, he is lying to himself. "By this do we know that we love God (and do not merely say so): if we have love for one another" (John 13:34–35).

In speaking of love in English, we face a grave disadvantage because we are accustomed to over-relying on the one word *love*. By contrast, in Latin and Greek, our forebears regularly had access to seven or eight words to express different kinds (and stages) of love. Among these are terms such as *amor, eros, affectus, philia, dilectio, amicitia, agape* and *caritas*.

To come to the full meaning of caritas, it helps tremendously to come to a good understanding of each of the other stages of love. Each one adds to our knowledge of the highest—caritas. All these different loves begin in God, and all return back to Him. Where they are, God is.

The most general sort of love is amor—the term Dante used for the force that moves the sun and choreographs the stars in their millennial dance across the skies. Amor means pull, attraction, being driven together. One can use it of Earth's gravity or the passions that pull the sexes to cohabit.

But eros is a love more obsessive, almost mad. It is the "boundless desire" described by the great Swiss lay theologian Denis de Rougemont as "'a divine delirium,' a transport of the soul, a madness . . . the supreme soaring of desire." A young man stricken by eros cannot get the image of the woman who is his current passion out of his mind. Even if he is with his favorite family members or best friends, his mind is fixed on her—looking for a text message, eager to telephone her. Even if he has nothing to say, just to have contact. A young woman may be so obsessed with a man that she tries to show up anywhere she might cross his path—signs up for the same classes, perhaps.

Eros may also drive the intellect, not only the heart. It is a hunger to discover knowledge, to keep asking questions. The one possessed by this eros for understanding may go without eating or without getting up from her desk or library stack, unaware of time passing or hunger pressing.

What distinguishes eros is its drivenness. Eros is not simply an attraction or a beating heart, such as amor kindles. Eros is a kind of madness, a lack of balance, an inability—or almost an inability—to calm one's passion, to channel it, to slow it down, or to keep it in perspective with other goals and with a sense of all the years left to go forward gradually. "Easy does it," sings Frank Sinatra. But to slow down eros is by no means easy. Nearly all contemporary love songs—not all, but a great many—are about eros.

The third term is affectus—a term referring to feelings of admiration for our beloved and a desire to be with her, feelings of compatibility and comfort, feelings that tend to have a longer run than hot passions and yield in daily life a quieter security. Think of a kitten purring with contentment in your lap.

The Greek term philia lifts eros to a more stable and restful level, to the kind of friendship worthy of lifelong marriage. The term dilectio introduces a more restricted notion, one of a love born of deliberation and reflective choice. Dilectio comes from, but intensifies, the root *electio* (choice). It is a love born by singling out one friend, for some high degree of commitment: We will be friends forever, and you are the one I choose to love forever. Dilectio can be relied upon because it is deliberate; it follows from a weighing of the consequences. I am not swept off my feet. It is the love of careful, reflective choice. It is the love on which friendship is built.

The term amicitia adds to dilectio the note of mutuality. If you have ever loved anyone who did not reciprocate that love, you know the pain caused by the lack of mutuality. All the more, you appreciate the gift of love that someone freely makes when she returns the love you offer. Mutual love, amicitia (friendship), is far more powerful than any love, save one.

Typically, agape is used for the love for humans shown by the Father in sending his only Son into the world in human form. As de Rougemont has written in his classic book, *Love in the Western World*:

"And the Word was made flesh, and dwelt among us, (and we beheld his glory, the glory as of the only begotten of the Father,) full of grace and truth." The incarnation of the Word in the world—and of Light in Darkness—is the astounding event whereby we are delivered from the woe of being alive. And this event, in being the centre of the whole of Christianity, is the focus of that Christian love which in Scripture is called agape.

Agape is, further, the term used for Christ's willingness to sacrifice Himself and die for our restoration into the love of His Father. Agapic love signifies a will to sacrifice oneself. Agape emphasizes the dimension of suffering on behalf of another, as in "to lay down one's life for one's brother." ("Greater love than this no man has.")

Caritas is the origin of all loves. It exists in the inner life of God Himself, a calmer, transcendent form of love. Caritas is alive in God, so to speak, even "before" the agape of Jesus Christ upon the cross.

The crucial point here is that the fullest of these loves is the one that we do not have in our nature, the one that is unmerited and unattainable through our own efforts—the one that is the greatest of God's gifts to us, a sharing in His own inner life. The name of that love, infused in us from outside our nature (though it is not contrary to our nature), needs and has its own special name: caritas. It is the love of God poured out through us, the Love by which we love others as God does, not merely as we could love them all by ourselves. From this love comes a love that is unnatural: "Love your enemies." Let God do that through you.

In the here and now, in this place, at this time, God needs your voice and ours, our eyes and our hands to show His love for all His children on this earth. He diffuses His love into us and through us to all others. We are to be the vessels of His love. He made the world a means of transmitting His love through such imperfect conduits as us.

Here—in caritas—lies the heart of the lay vocation. Here lies its inner energy. Here lies its more-than-human power. Here lies its outward-streaming dynamism. Laypeople are called to take the Lord's love to all the nooks and crannies on earth, all those places where priests may not be, and to reach (in the end) every last person on earth, especially among the poor and the suffering.

God is love. God sends love through us to the neighbors among whom we find ourselves. Especially those who get under our skin. (The nice ones are easy to love, using our own resources. It is in the struggle to love the unpleasant, even repulsive, that we call upon God's love outpoured within us.) St. Thérèse prays for those annoying her: "As soon as I am aware of them, I pray for those people the thought of whom is diverting my attention, and in this way they reap the benefits from my distractions . . . I accept all for the love of God, even the wildest fancies that cross my mind."

The mission of the layperson is to diffuse God's fiery caritas to all the world, beginning exactly where we are, among those He has committed to our personal care. We are to love them as God loves them. Better, we are to let them experience God's love through what we do and say and feel.

At this task, we all fall short and often ultimately fail. Yet God's caritas is unfailingly present (if behind the darkening clouds). We desperately hope that He supplies for our lack and touches our neighbors directly with His warmth.

CHAPTER 16

Looking Inward

"If you do not know how to meditate on heavenly things, direct your thoughts to Christ's passion and willingly behold His sacred wounds. If you turn devoutly to the wounds and precious stigmata of Christ, you will find great comfort in suffering, you will mind but little the scorn of men, and you will easily bear their slanderous talk."

—THOMAS À KEMPIS,
THE IMITATION OF CHRIST

How is the layperson to radiate to others the good news of the Gospel if he or she has not yet internally absorbed and assimilated that good news? All apostolic work begins inside oneself. In fact, emphasis on the interior life is one of the most distinctive features of the way of living taught us by Jesus Christ. Not the outside of the cup, but the inside. Not the prayers on our lips, but the prayers in our hearts and minds.

But who is there to teach us how to live the interior life? Where in this busy world does anyone even call to public attention the fact that that there is a desperate need for living an interior life?

To pursue such a life, it is necessary to imbibe the four Gospels slowly, a little every day, with two purposes in mind. One is to allow their rich words and images to steep in one's mind. The second is to fall in love with Jesus Christ, the axial figure of all human history, the One, the man who connects us with the Creator of all things, His Father. He who taught us to pray: "Our Father, who art in heaven . . ." Who showed us how to order our desires: "Father, not my will, but Thine be done." The exemplar of how we are to live and to die: "Father, into Thy hands I commend my spirit."

To fall in love with Jesus Christ is to fall in love with the most other-transforming human being—the most extraordinary being—who ever lived. It is at the same time to fall in love with the Word (the blazing flash of insight) "in Whom, and by Whom, and with Whom were made all the things that were made." He is, as Dante wrote, "the Love that moves the sun and all the stars." He is united totally with His Father, and all those who are one with Him are also one with the Father.

To fall in love with Jesus Christ is to learn how He spoke and acted, to meditate on His manner and His way, to soak up His thoughts, His silences, His gestures, in order to draw their meaning into our hearts. No layperson is going to live out her (or his) vocation unless she "puts on Jesus Christ" and allows Him to warm those around her with His love. She must follow the encouragement of St. Paul to "put on the mind of Christ" until it is "no longer she, but He, who lives in her."

No one, of course, does this very well. Our faults and the odd angles of our personalities get in the way. Yet we are called to do the best we can to let Christ live within us, to let Christ act within us, to let Christ communicate through us His love for others.

This is the first step in living the interior life: we must begin paying more attention to the Gospels, allowing them to transform us from within, to alter our interior being—our hearts, our minds, our souls—in such a way that the fire of Christ, however dim its embers within us, radiates outward in our external life. We must first attend to what is within, then to what flows outward. Attend first to the Kingdom of God, which, as Jesus has said, is within us (Luke 17:20–21). Nourish that weak inner flicker.

To accomplish this, for most of us, means learning how to withdraw from the outer world that until now has so much engaged us, occupied our minds, filled us with cares, given us diversion. It means learning how to withdraw from the world of busyness "and come apart into the desert a while" (Mark 6:31).

One crucial habit to learn is to bring periods of silence into our lives, periods of quiet and internal rest, in contemplation of the mysteries of God's ways and works. One needs to learn how to be still. To take time to drop all other cares. To sit in the silent, unseen, sometimes dry presence of God.

It helps also to practice throughout the day—perhaps seven times a day (a metaphorical number)—by pausing to meditate on an incident from the Gospel. Morning, noon, and night are obvious times. But so are mealtimes, or perhaps they are more suited to a three-minute pause, midmorning and midafternoon. (More on this theme will be found in the next chapter.)

Some people have been helped by practicing "custody" of their eyes, taste, touch, and other senses. That is, instead of simply letting the five senses be called hither and yon by various stimuli, they pause to reflect and choose deliberately how to direct them. For example, while working at one's desk, one may deliberately confine one's field of vision to the area within the edges of the desk. This practice helps concentration.

Many people take care to confine the roving of their eyes as they return from Holy Communion at Mass. Others, before taking a quick sip of water when they are thirsty, like to pause for a moment to make the sip deliberate, and they turn it into a silent prayer of gratitude. In other words, instead of living a life driven solely by sensory stimuli, many have learned to bring "our friends, the senses" under the sweet suasion of our hearts and minds. This effort leads to a kind of wholeness of body and soul.

Father John Jay Hughes of St. Louis once used this example in a homily: a stranger entered a cafeteria and, finding no empty tables, asked a man if he might sit down with him. The other said, "Sure," and then, before eating, bowed his head to say grace. The stranger then mocked him: "I never do that. I figure I earn my bread by the sweat of my brow. I owe nothin' to nobody. So I just plunge in and eat."

The man who had said grace agreed, without animus. "I have a dog who does the same thing."

Living an interior life is essentially a matter of turning even one's bodily actions into a gesture of thanksgiving and learning to live in wholeness of soul and body—rather than as if the body were separate from the soul, and the soul from the body.

In our kind of world, so full of distractions, it is at first difficult to learn to live quietly within oneself. But many actually learn such habits, much to the increased peace of their souls and to the delight of their bodies. The purpose of such inwardness is to form one's mind and heart in the mind, spirit, and actions of Christ. It is, very slowly, to become "another Christ."

CHAPTER 17

Into the Presence of God

"True peace of heart, then, is found in resisting passions, not in satisfying them. There is no peace in the carnal man, in the man given to vain attractions, but there is peace in the fervent and spiritual man."

—THOMAS À KEMPIS,
THE IMITATION OF CHRIST

"There was a lovely painting of Jesus above the altar." Above it was the verse "For lo, I am with you always." Just seeing that, "I had this really profound sense of the presence of God."
—FROM THE PROFILE OF CAMBRIA SMITH

An occasional awareness of being in the presence of God characterizes almost all the human beings who have ever lived. Before the modern age, this sense was well nigh universal. Even today, at the high tide of secularism in the parts of the world that are media saturated, the vast majority of human beings elsewhere on this planet are aware of God's presence through their reflections on their own experience.

The most famous public philosopher in Europe, Jürgen Habermas, was challenged to a debate on religion and society by then Cardinal Ratzinger just a few years ago. There and in other lectures, Habermas said he felt as if he had been awakened by September 11, 2001. Until then, he had thought that European secularism was the cutting edge of human progress and that, inevitably, the world would turn secular. After September 11, secular Europe seemed to him an island in the midst of a turbulent and growing sea of religion. The energy of history seemed to him to be with religion, not secularism.

Nonetheless, many Catholics in America have only an infrequent and dim awareness of God's presence. Keeping that awareness before our inner eye takes deliberate effort. The hurry of daily life keeps our attention fully occupied. We need to pay attention to what we are doing even in the small details of daily life: shaving, combing out our hair, straightening our clothes before going out the door, thinking about all we have to do during the day.

In my grandparents' time, life was far slower, and there were lots of extra minutes for living inwardly. Today, we begin each day with lists of all the varied things we have to accomplish: pick up Stephen or Emily, take them to music practice or sports, do the grocery shopping, get the front two rooms cleaned, do the laundry, put dinner on early since Emily has a recital at 7 o'clock. And a lot more than that.

Awareness of being with God, and of God's surrounding us, tends to get squeezed out. But how can active lay Catholics give God to others if they do not nourish Him within their own hearts night and day?

As in every other area of life, regular exercise makes a huge difference in performance. Take a look at some exercises for beginners—well, actually, for everybody. After lots of repetition, these things become second nature. People who have practiced them for some time do not need to think about them; they find themselves doing them for the pleasure of it.

1. In the first moments after getting up, maybe when brushing your teeth, ask God to accept every breath you take during the day to come as a prayer. Tell Him you mean every thought and action of the day to be a prayer. Ask Him to help you all through the day to think of His presence.

2. Choose another action that comes just a few moments after that—kissing your children, or pausing for a quick hug from your spouse as you part for the day, or perhaps the moment of turning your car keys in the ignition or looking in the rearview mirror—and say another little prayer. Offer the day to Him again. Ask Him to take care of all of you all through the day. Pray for the needy, those who suffer, those who fight for life. Just a fleeting thought will do, just to remind yourself of the immense spiritual struggle going on all around you and to attune your own inner heart to that struggle in your own life.

3. You probably know some people for whom sipping coffee suggests a morning cigarette. Good habits are also formed by making spontaneous, habitual connections. Every time you hear a bird sing, every time you hear a bell ring, remind yourself that God is within you, and all around you, and especially in all the people you will meet that day—most notably in the difficult and unpleasant ones.

4. Every time you hear a police or ambulance siren, say a swift prayer for those who may be suffering terribly at that moment and ask God to be with them and to be present to you too. Unite your own life to their suffering, in the suffering of Jesus on the cross, all of us, one.

5.   When you are impatient, stuck waiting in line or in traffic, make the very most of this time by recalling God's presence, with gratitude.

6.   "Where there is charity and love, there God is." All day long, every time you see an act of affection, friendship, or kindness, let it remind you that God is all around you. Where there is love, there God is. Moreover, love is contagious. The more of it you throw in the waters around you, the more caritas will ripple outward. Little smiles, and little pats on the back, go on until they go 'round the world and come back. Receiving kindness, people tend to pass it on. As Dostoevsky wrote, there is an invisible current of "humble charity" circling around this planet, moving love from one place to another.

6.   Another exercise is to think often of the biblical adage that you are "made in the image of God." God is infinite, so in order to reflect all the facets of His beauty, an infinite number of humans are needed (so to speak), each to reflect a fragment of His loveliness. If one of these humans is eliminated, that facet of God's beauty is missing. The image of God is disfigured. That is one more reason why it is so awful to harm another human being.

The consequence is that each time we meet a human being, even an unpleasant one, we are invited to look more carefully, to see if we can discern what is most beautiful somewhere within him (though it may need to be drawn out), that God placed there in love for him, and to render him a (perhaps hidden) image of Himself.

This habit makes every human being that we meet a reflection of God's radiant being, worthy of our attention and our love. Each human encounter also makes us aware of the presence of God. "How do we know that we love God?" St. John's Epistle asks. The test is a simple one. Just saying the words "I love you" is not enough. The key is this: "if you have love for one another."

Every human being brings us into the presence of God, for each is a living image of Him. For some reason, God sent that person to us as our "neighbor," a sign of His presence in our midst. I have sometimes found this hard to discern in some people. Some have found it hard to discern in me. The ones who are hard for us to love are the most important for us to love, for in loving them, we do not do so for our pleasure but for God's.

7.   At night, every writer of spiritual exercises suggests, we should reflect back on the day, to recall how steadily we have been in the presence of God and how we might have done better. Some people pick out one of their worst faults— impatience, maybe, or an uncontrolled temper—and resolve to diminish their appearance every day. Some days, a person does better than on other days. Most of our faults have deep roots, so digging them out entirely is very hard. The most important thing is perseverance, little by little. Take setbacks with good humor, and use failures as an occasion for throwing yourself on God's mercy. Mercy is our God's deepest desire. The best name for our God is "mercy," according to St. Thomas Aquinas. Be merciful to yourself, but resolute.

In addition to these exercises, we can find our way toward God by the path of beauty. Think of the vastness of the sky, the enormity of the seas covering two-thirds of the earth. The endless ranges of the Rockies. Crisp, cold mountain air. Sunsets in Mexico City, Iowa, the Delaware coast. Mozart's "Eine kleine Nachtmusik," sonatas of Haydn, Brahms. The language of Shakespeare and Dostoevsky . . . God has gifted us with countless instances of beauty, artistic and natural. He Who created these is more beautiful still.

Sometimes, God leaves us dry, as if our souls were in a desert, where the cistern is cracked and water runs no more through it. We cannot feel God's presence. There is no sweetness, no light. Our faith seems empty and a hoax. It is night in our souls. This night may go on for days, even months, sometimes entire years. St. Thérèse provides good counsel for such times: "I do not desire the thrill of love which I can feel; if Jesus feels its thrill, then that is enough for me."

These are the best of times. For now, we turn to God most purely and most like an adult. The sweets of childhood have been taken away. There is no more gladness or spontaneity in the soul. Our soul feels parched, dry, and leathery. But God is closest to us then, for we are no longer living by His comfort and consolation but by His agony in the garden and His dry thirst on the cross.

Wait for the moments of emptiness. Rejoice in them. At last, God is treating you as an adult. The kind of joy you will feel is also dark, different from any other joy. Consider again the words of St. Thérèse: "I give thanks to Jesus for making me walk in darkness, and in the darkness I enjoy profound peace." Union solely with God brings its own silent joy, apart from all illusion.

No one sees God. It is good not to see Him. It is right. It is fitting. God is not on the frequency of our senses. No one can touch Him with their hands or hear Him with their ears or taste or gain scent of Him. If we caught sight of Him, our fuses would blow out. They are not made for so much "wattage." Like a website overwhelmed, we would go dark.

It is important to learn the ways in this desert, to grasp the geography of the interior life, to become content in the darkness and the chill. The point is to turn our outside in. To change the balance of our attention span so that more and more is inward, lived in the light of eternity and the dear, dear God in Whose presence we live and move.

None of this will detract from our everyday work in the world. On the contrary, we will become sharper and more attentive to dimensions in it that we had not seen, and we will perform better than we did before. How could we not? The same God gave us our vocations, and Himself.

CHAPTER 18

The Sacraments

"If grace were always given at once, or were present at our beck and call, it would not be well taken by weak humankind. Therefore, with good hope and humble patience await the grace of devotion."

—THOMAS À KEMPIS,
THE IMITATION OF CHRIST

"If I ever exhaust the potential of my baptism, that would be one thing, but that has yet to happen. So I think I'm doing what I was initially baptized as a priest, prophet, and king to do."

—FROM THE PROFILE OF KATHLEEN KICHLINE

One of the distinguishing marks of the Catholic faith among the world religions is its belief in the resurrection. Resurrection, that is, not solely of the soul but of the body. Of both body and soul as one. True, at earthly death, the body decays and falls back into the earth, dust to dust; nonetheless, the messages coming to us from Jesus Christ include the affirmation that bodies and souls will be reunited, as is only fitting. For the human being proper is one in soul and body, an embodied soul or, perhaps, an ensouled body, both together as one person. Without our bodies, we are not ourselves. Without an animating soul, our bodies are spiritless and dead.

How will that resurrection be done? No one knows. But it is part of what Christ said is true. The empirical test comes in living. One day, we will know in experience what today we are convinced of only darkly.

There are two prayers in whose formulae this conviction is embedded, the longer Nicene Creed and the shorter Apostles' Creed. The Nicene Creed is said publicly at every Sunday Mass, in unison by the whole congregation, articulated by the voice of each person. At its end, this Creed, common to all Christians since the Church was born (but given formal shape only in AD 325), carries the concluding words: "We acknowledge one baptism for the forgiveness of sins. We look for the resurrection of the dead, and the life of the world to come. Amen."

This common Christian belief in the importance of the human body is taken with unusual seriousness by the Catholic people. The Catholic Church is deliberately more bodily, carnal, physical, and sensual than the churches descending from the Puritans or even from the reformers Luther and Calvin. This sensuality quite commonly has stunned those Protestants attending a Catholic Eucharist for the first time, as witnessed in this famous text from John Adams, when he first experienced a Catholic Mass in Philadelphia at the Congress of 1776:

> The dress of the priest was rich with lace—his pulpit was
> velvet and gold. The altar piece was very rich—little images
> and crucifixes about—wax candles lighted up. But how shall
> I describe the picture of our Savior in a frame of marble over

the altar at full length upon the Cross, in the agonies, and the blood dropping and streaming from his wounds?[*]

Colored glass, and color in sensuous paintings, incense, the Mass as a slow-motion dance, the sacred arts of sweet and soaring and lightsome music (classical and popular), the tastes of unleavened bread and special altar wine—every one of the five senses is brought into exercise and given pleasure.

In this sense, the Catholic faith takes incarnation seriously; the flesh matters greatly to it. If God the Father chooses to have His Son take flesh, He must choose between becoming either a woman or a man. There is no neutral, sexless possibility. Incarnation demands of God a choice of flesh. But what are the historical implications of the one choice or the other? If God were to become human by choosing to come as a female, what would that communicate without using words, what would it symbolize, how would it transform the culture of its time? If coming as a male, what does having a male body (and male drives and emotions, roles and duties) symbolize? What transformative power does that choice carry with it?

One of the effects of the choice for God to come as male rather than female was to throw down a challenge to the culture that had prevailed for the thousands of years that humans had trod the earth before the coming of Christ. During those thousands of years, the culture of the male was to train up as a warrior, while the culture of the female prepared her for nurturing the young and for dominance in the home. Of course, these early forms of male and female culture were subject to change as the conditions of life changed.

---

[*] Quoted in David McCullough, *John Adams* (New York: Simon & Schuster, 2001), 84.

The Catholic Church taught that a Christian warrior should be distinguished by "*charitée, courtesie,* and *chivalrie.*" For this teaching, Friedrich Nietzsche rightly accused the Church of "feminizing" the male warrior. The ideal set before a Christian civilization is not the man of ferocity but the gentle man, the man who reflects from his own actions and aspect the spirit of the tender Christ. There are many things the Christian knight will not do. There are rules, customs, prohibitions, points of honor. Christian civilizations aim to gentle the male animal and to steel the female to purposefulness, wisdom, suffering, fierce courage, and triumphant persistence (as Our Lady did). Women during the centuries of the Crusades ran nearly every estate in Europe as well as vast chains of convents and monasteries, chastised popes as did Catherine of Siena, and became Doctors of the Church. Christianity transformed the female as well as the male of the species.

By emphasizing the centrality of incarnation in human history—the difference that being male and being female makes to human development and their transformation to a new nobility and a new ideal for humankind—Christian civilizations transformed both the male and the female without confounding the strengths and potentialities of each.

The point is, during the first two millennia of its existence, the Church has studied the symbolic depths of the human body. Its art values both the male and the female bodies. Its Churches glory in the depiction of enfleshed, embodied, full-blooded persons in the great actions and decisive moments of their lives.

Catholic life begins with baptism, usually although far from always, the baptism of the infant, on whose tongue is placed a taste of the salt of hardship and who is bathed with the shock of water poured over its downy head (which usually induces an infant's cries of perturbation). Baptism also includes an anointing with oils, as if to prepare the infant for the lifetime battles of the athlete and the soldier. Meanwhile, godparents speak oaths confessing the basics of faith and in defiance of the Evil One in the name of the speechless child, and they hold candles kindled from the flame of the Paschal candle of the triumph over death of the radiant and risen Christ.

But the principle of incarnation is also lived out through the six other sacraments. What is a sacrament? In the most general sense, it is any material thing that pulls back the veils on the sacred—as a beautiful day in May can lift the heart to sing glory to God or a bad sermon or other tedium may call the mind to unavoidable suffering (the daily cross) that lies at the heart of all things large and small in human life. More precisely, in the good English words of the Council of Baltimore (1883), a sacrament is "an outward sign, instituted by Christ, to give grace," that is to say, to infuse in us the inner life of God. Put another way, a sacrament is the use of human flesh in imitation of Christ's divine life. For example, this life is infused in us through baptism, the Eucharist, holy orders, matrimony, the anointing of the ill with holy oils, the confession of sins, and the confirmation of young adults with the oil of imminent battle.

There are in all seven of these signs instituted by Christ, appropriate in their ensemble for every stage of human life. Sacraments bless us in our infant beginnings and also when we reach "the age of reason" (identified as more or less in bloom by the age of seven), and when we transition from childhood into adult maturity and warriorhood, against the forces of evil in every life.

At the age of reason, the sacraments of frequent nourishment begin to be taken: the sacrament of telling one's sins in whispers to an ordained confessor, as if telling them to God Himself, outside the easy self-deceptions of one's own interior. In this way, our internal restlessness about our sins is brought into the light of day, for comment and counsel by another trained to this purpose, who exacts repentance and a change of life and ends by giving God's own blessing.

And also the great sacrament of the Eucharist, in memory of the actions and promises of Christ Himself at the Last Supper, consecrating humble bread and ordinary wine into His own Body and Blood, the reality of the unity of all in one same meal—that is, of God and humans united down the ages and in the eyes of God into all eternity.

It is the part of Catholic men and women to partake often of the sacraments of telling their sins and repenting them, and of the breaking of the Bread, in order to unite themselves with God and to let His caritas flow through them. This is what they have to bring to the world. Here lies the inner dynamo from which inner longing flows into the bloodstream of the world.

CHAPTER 19

Imbibing the Wisdom of the Ages—Spiritual Readings for the Lay Catholic

"The more reflective and meditative prayer was a great way to unwind. These opportunities really put me in my spiritual niche."

—FROM THE PROFILE OF ELIAS MOO

There is no doubt that full concentration on the love of God, and the habit of prayer ("Pray always," in every instant of every day), are the most crucial elements of a fruitful Christian life. But the single best nourishment of prayer and love for God is sound, deep, quiet, considered reading of the works of great guides of the soul.

In the first thousand years of the history of the Christian Church, as in the thousands of years of Jewish history, the heart of this reading was the Word of God in Scripture. Our forebears called this the *lectio divina*, divine reading, soaking one's mind in the Word of God, letting the soul absorb the Word of God. How else would we come to know what pleases God, unless we study what He has told us?

It must be remembered that for thousands of years, those who reflected deeply on prayer—and who were free by their conditions of life to spend nearly all day, every day, in prayer and study and writing—were monks and other particularly dedicated religious persons. But often, even they were among the very few literate and educated persons of their time (especially in the long centuries before the printing press). For this reason, it was often they who also had to lead armies, write laws, and imagine and create and run civic institutions. They may have been consecrated religious persons, but they by necessity also took on very active secular, lay roles. They too needed to learn how to pray in the midst of very busy, detailed lay work.

When I, Michael, think back over my own 60 years of spiritual reading and 50 years of active lay life, I recall with special fondness a half-dozen or so authors who were of abiding help to me. I have been driven back to their work again and again. Always there is nourishment there.

Some of these books use the language of the monastery, as in a line like "go back to your cell in solitude," when what they mean may be as simple as "withdraw your mind inwardly a bit, be alone with yourself a moment, take stock, rest with God, take a deep breath of God." In other words, attend to your inner life, not just your outward life. Both are one, outer and inner. But the outer one has the habit of making more noise and stirring more emotion and arousing strong passions. To keep in touch with the inner life takes much more practice. The outward life all too quickly fascinates and absorbs us, demands less of us. It is too often an escape and a distraction.

There are many writers who are more contemporary than the ones we like best. But these are rarely as deep and lasting. In fact, the contemporary writers have usually acquired what depth they have by learning from the classical writers. Contemporary writers (like me) burn out like meteorites. The classics endure across the generations. "When you have a choice, choose the classics," someone once told me. I don't remember who, but I often breathe a word of thanks to him.

Thomas Merton was an activist layman until he felt seized by a call to full-time prayer and study among the Trappists. His autobiography *The Seven Storey Mountain* was almost mandatory reading for my generation. His *Seeds of Contemplation* and other books were aimed at teaching those of us in lay life how to pray with the ancient wisdom acquired by the monks and nuns down the ages, who made prayer their full-time occupation.

Recently, I was being driven to a lecture by a young laywoman who said quietly to me that she loves to pray. She prays three or four hours every day, she told me, and would love to do more, if she could. So Thomas Merton was quite right in imagining that there are legions of laypeople who hunger to know more than they do about prayer. Now monks are not the only literate and learned ones. Millions of laypeople have higher schooling too. They need to sharpen their minds and go out exploring into the night where no one sees God, and they need guides and teachers.

Here are some passages from a shorter book Merton wrote called *Life and Holiness*, just for a taste. The idea is to read each of them. Pause. Read again. Let them soak in. That is how spiritual reading is best done. It is a bit different from other reading. It is not just for information. It is for feeding and shaping the soul. It is for making its insights a part of your own inner life. It is for changing our own inner life. Not just to read and forget, but to let it get under the skin, go inside, become a forming influence. Here, then, is one set of pearls from Merton:

> If we are called by God to holiness in life, and if holiness is beyond our natural power to achieve (which it certainly is), then it follows that God himself must give us the light, the

strength, and the courage to fulfill the task he requires of us. He will certainly give us the grace we need. If we do not become saints it is because we do not avail ourselves of his gift.

Our time needs more than devout, church-going people who avoid serious wrongs (or at least the wrongs that are easily recognized for what they are) but who seldom do anything constructive or positively good. It is not enough to be outwardly respectable. On the contrary, mere external respectability, without deeper or more positive moral values, brings discredit upon the Christian faith.

If we are to be "perfect" as Christ is perfect, we must strive to be as perfectly human as he . . . Hence sanctity is not a matter of being less human, but more human than other men. This implies a greater capacity for concern, for suffering, for understanding, for sympathy, and also for humor, for joy, for appreciation of the good and beautiful things of life.

To love is to be fully committed to the Church's work of salvation, the renewal and dedication of man and his society to God. No Christian can remain unconcerned in this work. Today, the dimensions of the task are as wide as the world itself.

Each one becomes perfect, not by realizing one uniform standard of universal perfection in his own life, but by responding to the call and the love of God, addressed to him within the limitations and circumstances of his own peculiar vocation.

In Christian sanctity, a certain human weakness and imperfection are altogether compatible with the perfect love of God, as long as one acquires humility from the experience of one's own wretchedness and thus learns to place an ever more total and perfect trust in the grace of God.

For . . . true lovers of God, all things, whether they appear good or evil, are in actuality good. All things manifest the loving mercy of God. All things enable them to grow in love. All events serve to unite them closer to God. For such men obstacles no longer exist. God has turned even obstacles into means to their ends, which are also his own.

The second book of spiritual reading we have found exceedingly helpful, even for opening at random and accepting what Providence shows us, is *The Imitation of Christ*, a classic first published in 1418. In the past 600 years, no one has published a better way to learn concrete things to do during each day in order to shape one's own inner life to be more like that of Jesus Christ. "To put on the mind of Christ" was the deepest wish of the Apostle Paul. This is the most marvelous how-to book ever written on the subject. One reason it is has remained fresh for so many centuries is that it concentrates on the inner life more than on outward circumstances.

The *Imitation* author was Thomas à Kempis, born near Cologne, Germany, in about 1380, an affable young priest, scholar, and writer much influenced by the revival among laypeople in the Lowlands who tried to live as much like the first Christians of Jerusalem and Antioch as possible.

Our guide Thomas divides his book into four parts: thoughts helpful to the life of the soul, the interior life, internal consolation, and an invitation to the Eucharist. His is not a book to be read once. Each time one reads it, one discovers in it new wisdom and new answers to questions one at first didn't even know how to ask. To put on the mind of Christ is a lifetime's work.

Perhaps it might nourish our souls to taste, thoughtfully and with open hearts, the advice young Thomas offered us, based on his own experience.

It is vanity to wish for long life and to care little about a well-spent life. It is vanity to be concerned with the present only and not to make provision for things to come. It is vanity to love what passes quickly and not to look ahead where eternal joy abides.

When a man of good will is afflicted, tempted, and tormented by evil thoughts, he realizes clearly that his greatest need is God, without Whom he can do no good. Saddened by his miseries and sufferings, he laments and prays.

No man deserves the consolation of heaven unless he persistently arouses himself to holy contrition. If you desire true sorrow of heart, seek the privacy of your cell and shut out the uproar of the world, as it is written: "In your chamber bewail your sins." There you will find what too often you lose abroad.

If you do not know how to meditate on heavenly things, direct your thoughts to Christ's passion and willingly behold His sacred wounds. If you turn devoutly to the wounds and precious stigmata of Christ, you will find great comfort in suffering, you will mind but little the scorn of men, and you will easily bear their slanderous talk.

When consolation is taken away, do not at once despair but wait humbly and patiently for the heavenly visit, since God can restore to you more abundant solace.

THE VOICE OF CHRIST: MY CHILD, I will teach you now the way of peace and true liberty. Seek, child, to do the will of others rather than your own. Always choose to have less rather than more. Look always for the last place and seek to be beneath all others. Always wish and pray that the will of God be fully carried out in you. Behold, such will enter into the realm of peace and rest.

In one short moment God often gives what He has long denied. At times He grants at the end what He has denied from the beginning of prayer. If grace were always given at once, or were present at our beck and call, it would not be well taken by weak humankind. Therefore, with good hope and humble patience await the grace of devotion.

God, eternal, incomprehensible, and infinitely powerful, does great and inscrutable things in heaven and on earth, and there is no searching into His marvelous works. If all the works of God were such that human reason could easily grasp them, they would not be called wonderful or beyond the power of words to tell.

To write about spiritual reading, of course, is actually to address the subjects that those readings dwell on. So it is a good way to talk about several substantive topics too, not just to recommend readings.

For example, there is the difficult subject of prayer—a practical guide about how to do it, the different types of prayer, and the different exercises one can do to learn to pray in each of these ways.

There is also the subject of how contemplation and meditation—growing out of the slow, absorptive reading that leads quietly into prayer—are related to action, especially practical action for the People of God, that is, for the Church in all its mundane tasks. Of what use are these worldly actions if they do not give off eternal resonance?

Allow us then to introduce a few more writers whose work is of extraordinary assistance in learning how to live a lively inner life. There are two great women writers, Doctors of the Church both of them, St. Teresa of Avila and St. Thérèse of Lisieux.

In travels all around the world, Michael has found only one or two churches that did not have among the statues of saints around their walls a statue of St. Thérèse. She must be among the most beloved of all saints. Her teaching is stated with great simplicity, and also depth. Her book *The Story of a Soul* is filled with sound advice, especially about how to exercise an ever-fuller love for God and your immediate neighbors, your co-workers, members of your own family. Here are a few passages from that autobiographical work:

If all the lowly flowers wished to be roses, nature would lose its springtide beauty, and the fields would no longer be enamelled with lovely hues. And so it is in the world of souls, Our Lord's living garden. He has been pleased to create great Saints who may be compared to the lily and the rose, but He has also created lesser ones, who must be content to be daisies or simple violets flowering at His Feet, and whose mission it is to gladden His Divine Eyes when He deigns to look down on them. And the more gladly they do His Will the greater is their perfection.

I can truly say that Suffering opened her arms to me from the first, and I took her to my heart . . . As Our Lord made me understand that it was by the Cross He would give me souls, the more crosses I met with, the stronger grew my attraction to suffering . . . This was precisely the flower I wished to offer to Jesus, a hidden flower which keeps its perfume only for Heaven.

Though my suffering seemed to have reached its height, yet my attraction thereto did not grow less, and soon my soul shared in the trials my heart had to bear. My spiritual aridity increased, and I found no comfort either in Heaven or on earth; yet, amid these waters of tribulation that I had so thirsted for, I was the happiest of mortals.

As for St. Teresa, the woman who excelled in unstoppable determination, few have ever written so well about the inner life, within which, in silence and often in darkness and aridity, the soul learns to discern the will of God and to love God in the darkness of unseeing. Read especially her *Soliloquies*. One single quote may whet your eagerness to take her as a guide. She was the great inspirer and teacher of St. Thérèse and, a century later, Mother Teresa of Calcutta.

> Oh, my soul! Let the will of God be done; this suits you.
> Serve and hope in His mercy, for He will cure your grief
> when penance for your faults will have gained some pardon
> for them. Don't desire joy but suffering. O true Lord and my
> King! I'm still not ready for suffering if Your sovereign hand
> and greatness do not favor me, but with these I shall be able
> to do all things.

In our day, when relativism is so rampant and love of material pleasures has so dulled the soul, the tendency to find emptiness in the place where God used to be is very pronounced. That is why we need teachers of prayer who understand this darkness and this emptiness, who embrace human suffering. God exceeds the "frequencies" on which our senses broadcast; our senses cannot find Him. In fact, any person who would look on God directly would be overpowered by blinding light and the deafening ring of emptiness. If you want to go to the God who exceeds the capacities of our senses, you must go by a dark way empty of our senses. St. Teresa, like her friend and teacher St. John of the Cross, are our people's best guides in a century like ours, an age of being and nothingness, formlessness, blindness, deafness.

Let us now turn to a number of writers far less well known, whose ability to penetrate to the heart of the mystery is extraordinary. These are writers you have perhaps never heard of. They are North Stars, as if intended for dark times like ours. We are thinking of a marvelous, very tiny book called *Abandonment to Divine Providence*. This book immediately issues a sharp challenge. Are you willing to throw yourself completely—now—

into the Lord's will, inscrutable as it often is? Are you willing to trust completely? Are you willing to let go?

Short as it is, the book is full of practical lessons about how to learn to trust, how to taste the dark and often bitter pleasures of throwing ourselves upon the daily, minute-by-minute will of God.

> All I want is for you to carry on as you are doing and endure what you have to do—but change your attitude to all these things. And this change is simply to say "I will" to all that God asks. What is easier? For who could refuse obedience to a will so kind and so good? By this obedience we shall become one with God.

✠

> If we have abandoned ourselves, there is only one rule for us: the duty of the present moment. The soul is as light as a feather, as fluid as water, simple as a child and as lively as a ball in responding to all the impulses of grace. We are like molten metal which takes the shape of the mold into which it is poured, and can just as easily assume any form God wishes to give us.

This is the essence of the matter, isn't it? Isn't it the secret to the life of Mary the Mother of God? "Be it done to me according to Thy Word." Isn't it the secret to the life of our Lord? "Not my will, but Thine be done." It may be impossible to understand what is happening in our lives. But it is not impossible to trust the Lord Who throws you into what you cannot understand.

Then there is that wise and wonderful Irish monk of the 20th century, Eugene Boylan, who bequeathed to us two exceedingly lovely books: *This Tremendous Lover* and *Difficulties in Mental Prayer*. Because prayer in the mind (in imagination and, finally, in intellect) is so crucial to the fruitfulness of our actions and the integrity of our lives—so crucial and yet so difficult—here are two very helpful hints of his.

> Be it noted that God often gives during the day, even in our most active moments, the graces that He withheld during the time of prayer. In fact, for a soul who takes care to accept and to adapt himself to all the workings of God's Providence, especially when He seems to set obstacles in its path, His ways, however unreasonable they may seem at first, are in fact full of a most wonderful tenderness and merciful bounty.

> Above all, the absolute and essential necessity of humility for progress in prayer should be emphasized. God made the world for His own glory, and He will not give His glory to another . . . All the works of our supernatural life come from Him.

Dom Jean-Baptiste Chautard was a very busy abbot, forced by circumstances to be active in worldly and practical things, and so he was especially serious about finding ways to infuse his activities with the strength of the Gospels. What is the sense of pretending to build up the Church in practical ways, if there is no soul in it? The fire of the Gospels is the crucial element in Christian action. Dom Chautard set down his highly useful reflections in *The Soul of the Apostolate*, another very short book. One tiny morsel:

> No matter what my condition may be, if I am only willing to pray and become faithful to grace, Jesus offers me every

means of returning to an interior life that will restore to me my intimacy with Him, and will enable me to develop His life in myself. And then, as this life gains ground within me, my soul will not cease to possess joy, even in the thick of trials.

There is one last prayer we cannot conclude this chapter without. It is a prayer that Michael's wife liked so much, she had it framed for their front hallway and sent other framed copies to their children. It is a tough prayer. It had to be, because Karen suffered all her life from what Winston Churchill called "black dog"—a congenital tendency toward depression, triggered in recurrent cycles by the tiniest of setbacks or failures. She very often was plunged into emptiness, darkness, and even the physical pain of intense despair. Perhaps these few words (which, for those who have studied her paintings and prints, would not need to be spoken) will help to explain the comfort and guidance that St. John of the Cross often brought to her, as they have to many down the ages.

> In order to arrive at having pleasure in everything,
> Desire to have pleasure in nothing.
> In order to arrive at possessing everything,
> Desire to possess nothing.
> In order to arrive at being everything,
> Desire to be nothing.
> In order to arrive at that wherein thou hast no pleasure,
> Thou must go by a way wherein thou hast no pleasure.
>
> In order to arrive at that which thou knowest not,
> Thou must go by a way wherein thou knowest not.
> In order to arrive at that which thou possessest not,

Thou must go by a way that thou possessest not.
In order to arrive at that which thou art not,
Thou must go through that which thou art not.

Karen was not afraid of the dark. She accepted it as a friend and teacher. She hated the suffering it brought her. But she welcomed it as a necessary condition for coming closer to the Vision.

CHAPTER 20

Getting away from It All— Spiritual Retreats

Although "coming apart with the Lord to rest a while in prayer" is as old as the Bible, in our own time, the kind, variety, and number of retreats offered in every part of America year in, year out may be the most expansive in history. One thing we don't do as well in the United States as European nations still do is sponsor pilgrimages—especially long ones, by foot, over many days, and usually entailing some sleep-out nights under the stars. But retreats for a weekend, a week, or even a month are available in abundance and for every different lay need imaginable.

A quick Google search will turn up thousands of retreats for lay Catholics. If you search under your own diocese, you will find scores of possibilities. Every religious order and lay group seems to sponsor retreats, and there are many "retreat houses" that offer retreats all year round.

Parishes, schools, and all sorts of religious organizations find such retreats indispensable to allowing their members to renew their own interior lives, to reflect for a few days on where they are going spiritually and how their progress in overcoming faults and practicing new virtues is coming along.

The foundation stone of all retreats is much common prayer, often all together but in silence, sometimes aloud as in the traditional praying of the divine hours, sometimes along with a mix of lectures, sermons, and discussion periods. Almost always, a few hours of silent time at work in the gardens or in taking long walks around the grounds are built into the schedule.

The idea really is "retreat," to break up the routines of many months and to let the soul find some time to commune with God's presence, asking divine light on what to do next with one's life. Almost always, daily Mass is offered, and there are plenty of opportunities for the confession of one's sins and some private spiritual direction.

We have been trying to avoid offering a laundry list of the opportunities available. But we can think of no other way to suggest the breadth and depth of the possibilities, and to indicate the broad new scope of lay life today, than by listing six or seven interesting examples we came upon in our research.

In some ways, it is as if many special exercises and practices once chiefly available to those in religious vows or in studies for the priesthood or sisterhood have now become available to laypersons. The religious practice of the Catholic Church has rather quickly broadened, deepened, and become more various, in new centers of intensity.

The majority of retreats in the United States are made at retreat centers, and these are usually affiliated with particular dioceses. Let's begin with a few of the more specialized offerings in the Archdiocese of Washington, D.C., which may give us a small but representative taste of the variety of retreats available throughout the country.

The Loyola Retreat House in Faulkner, Maryland, hosts an annual retreat for separated and divorced Catholics. Led by a priest, the weekend is conceived as "a time to pause and reflect on being alive and well and turning our defeat into victory." The serene setting and the camaraderie of people sharing similar life experiences help individuals refocus and "reconnect" with God. Many who participate return year after year.

Our Lady of Mattaponi Retreat Center in Upper Marlboro, Maryland, offers a variety of family and youth retreats year-round. One especially popular program is the eighth-grade pregraduation retreat, which gives students an opportunity to conclude their grade-school experience and prepare for high school by reflecting on their faith and the important role it plays in their lives. Other specialized programs at Our Lady of Mattaponi include parish ministry retreats, days of recollection, confirmation retreats, and retreats for Hispanic young adults.

At the Center for Family Development, administered by the Legionaries of Christ in Bethesda, Maryland, retreat programs focus on marriage preparation, newlyweds, and marriage enrichment. Offerings also include mornings and evenings of recollection for men and for women, as well as retreats based on St. Ignatius's Spiritual Exercises.

For more than 40 years, the Dominican Retreat in McLean, Virginia, has sponsored some of the more creative and intriguing retreat options in the United States. Consider these one-day retreats, for example: "A Fresh Look at Fasting," "God Walks among the Pots & Pans," "Lessons from the Mystics," "The Spirituality of Sports," and "How Friends Help Us Get to Heaven." There is also a bimonthly program on "Centering Prayer," weekend retreats for members of Alcoholics Anonymous and Al-Anon, and Advent and Lenten days of prayer. Additionally, the Dominican Retreat offers spiritual direction as well as extended private retreats scheduled on an individual basis.

The largest and perhaps one of the most popular retreat venues in the country, the Malvern Retreat House in Malvern, Pennsylvania, reports that since its opening in 1922, it has hosted more than 1 million participants. In addition to traditional men's and women's programs, it offers, among other things, Ave Maria Singles retreats, an annual healing retreat, and a Valentine's Evening of Reflection, in which married couples renew their wedding vows, attend Mass, and enjoy an inspirational talk and candlelight dinner.

In addition to those administered by retreat centers, a range of programs are coordinated and overseen by national organizations. For example, Rachel's Vineyard Ministries is a source for women and men seeking post-abortion healing retreats. Its website offers a comprehensive listing of dates and locations of programs nationwide.*

Cornerstone is another national retreat movement. These annual weekend retreats are led by teams of laypeople who encourage participants to examine their life and their relationship with God more closely by sharing their own reflections on the role of faith in their life. A priest also offers the sacraments and is available for spiritual guidance. Faith-sharing in small-group settings is the emphasis of Cornerstone. After completing retreats, participants often form teams or small groups that continue to meet for spiritual fellowship and organized service projects.

The Cursillo Movement and the related ACTS Movement (Adoration, Community, Theology, and Service) are lay initiatives with an international presence, focused on training laypeople for effective leadership in parish service. Cursillo was founded in 1944 by a group of laymen in Majorca, Spain, and came to North America in 1957. The highly structured

---

* See www.rachelsvineyard.org.

weekend retreats, centered on 15 talks given by laypeople and priests, were originally Spanish-speaking only, but soon after arriving in the U.S., Cursillo retreats began being held in English. Today, nearly every U.S. diocese sponsors Cursillo retreats. The three-day format concludes with a turn to the "fourth day"—participants are encouraged to return to their daily lives, inspired to do service in their parishes and in the world. The ACTS Movement grew out of Cursillo in 1987 in the Archdiocese of San Antonio. ACTS retreats are similar in focus and structure, and they are also open to non-Catholic participants.

Beyond national organizations and movements, in an effort that truly transcends the limits of space and time, Online Ministries of Creighton University offers new possibilities in the form of "do-it-yourself" retreats; for example, the Creighton University Online Retreat for Everyday Life. A 34-week series of readings and meditations based on the movements of the Spiritual Exercises, this "user-friendly" self-guided retreat can be made individually or as a group. Participants are encouraged to keep a journal and to consult regularly with a spiritual director or a small group of others doing the same exercises. The Online Ministries interface also offers the opportunity to share personal reflections and insights in a forum on its website.

We have only just begun to scratch the surface. Anyone interested and ready to do even a few minutes of research will discover a seemingly boundless universe of opportunities for "coming apart with the Lord" on retreat. We hope you do.

CHAPTER 21

Are You Ready for Commitment? A Look at Oblates and Associates

*"'Know that it's not an easy road but there are others doing it.
Find a community of people . . . doing the same work you're
doing.' Being alone in this work can lead people to think that
'it's all about you.' But it's not. 'It's about what Christ does
through you.'"*

—FROM THE PROFILE OF ANSEL AUGUSTINE

*"The continuous and intimate presence of Jesus in our
hearts means that no place or occupation is an obstacle to
prayer . . . Not only is He already present wherever we may
be, but He is actually sharing our work—so that our work is
rather a means of prayer than an obstacle to it."*

—EUGENE BOYLAN,
DIFFICULTIES IN MENTAL PRAYER

Down through history, there have always been laypersons whose hearts burned to give more of themselves to the Lord. Laywomen and laymen followed the Lord as He preached and journeyed, sometimes for weeks on end. In later years, laymen around each Eucharistic community distributed food and medicine to needy neighbors. Still later, others founded orphanages, hospitals, and hospices. Laypeople built schools and took upon themselves the duties of teaching reading and writing and gradually the whole elementary basket of liberal arts. They did so in order that the young could better come to read and understand the Scriptures and to advance in the sciences and learning of their time. These schools trained musicians, painters, and sculptors.

Formal lay participation first sprouted up around monasteries—particularly Benedictine ones—from about AD 520 onward. And they encompass a whole world of spiritual pursuits—prayer and meditation; scholarship and the creation of beauty; care for the poor and the needy; aspiring toward the heavens in architecture; sculpture; printmaking; bronze ornaments; and music and painting.

It was not only the fully consecrated lives of the monks who were committed to these works of civilization. Gathered around them were also thousands of lay artisans, craftsmen, teachers, experts of various sorts, temporary or even lifetime volunteers who wanted to share in the work of the monks and other committed religious while still remaining laypersons.

At one time, in any medieval city in Europe, there might be hundreds of "lay oblates" and "lay associates" making the life of the monasteries full and thriving and expanding. The number of major European cities today that began life as villages gathered around monasteries is truly amazing. With the benefit of the monks' learning in botany, agriculture, livestock, sheep-raising, and other arts of agrarian life, the peasants living near monastery walls prospered, and from their new wealth, the great works of civilization multiplied in museums, libraries, exhibition halls, specialized schools, city fairs, and theaters.

In the 20th century, when war-torn Europe was trying to pull itself together from the devastations of modern barbarism, farsighted leaders designed a new medal to be awarded every year for great contributions to rebuilding a new European civilization. The image that won universal approval was the image of St. Benedict, whose scores (even hundreds) of lay-supported monasteries were the seedbeds of so many European cities and their achievements of great beauty and cultural aspiration.

Over the centuries, hundreds of thousands of laypersons associated themselves with the inner discipline and learning of the consecrated monks and in the practical crafts and inventions that continually improved the arts of daily life. The "industrial revolution of the 11th century" is sometimes singled out for its rich array of new inventions and technologies—in eyeglasses and telescopes; the stern rudder for ships; the shoulder harness that enabled horses and oxen to pull many times the weight they had formerly been able to pull; pulleys and iron devices for torquing up great pressures and lifting capacities; clocks and compasses; sundials for tracking the movements of the sun and other stars across the seasons, including whole sequences of shafts of light registering their movements across the walls and floors of great cathedrals. In addition to these, new arts were developed in metallurgy and in the seldom undersung or underappreciated arts of making beer, liqueur, and champagne. The monasteries were at the center, but the laypeople were an integral part of the work.

The Latin terms *oblate* and *oblation* suggest sacrifice. The new lay oblates were making a sacrifice of significant portions of their lives, in commitment to a morally and spiritually rigorous way of fulfilling their duties. They wished to distinguish themselves by new levels of Christian commitment, while retaining some of the benefits of living in a community and learning from the struggles and successes of their peers. "Wherever two or three are gathered in My Name, there am I in the midst of them." Being an oblate or a lay associate does seem to bring one closer to Christ in the spirit of small, intense communities.

But, of course, as the centuries rolled along, there were more and more "charisms" or special graces made manifest in dozens, scores, even hundreds of new religious communities. For example, the Dominicans' emphasis on the gifts of scholarship, preaching, and teaching, or the Franciscans' celebration of God's creation and special care for the poor. The distinctiveness of communities' charisms served to attract more and more laypeople to associate with particular communities. Each new religious order—the Dominicans, the Franciscans, later still the Jesuits, and the hundreds of smaller religious communities that flourished in the 18th and 19th centuries—developed its own style and methods for inviting lay associates into their work, at various levels of commitment.

The Catholic Church, a wise observer once remarked, is like a river shallow enough for an ant to wade through and deep enough for giraffes and elephants to drown in. It calls upon human beings of every sort of measure and talent and has work enough for each volunteer to perform to the best of their abilities. The Creator who first imagined and created humans in all their variety calls all of them to come serve their fellows in various ways. To these, there seems to be no limit to invention. Ever new possibilities seem to emerge with the novel needs of every successive generation.

In the past 30 years, lay association with religious communities has grown dramatically and evolved into myriad forms quite different from those of the centuries-old traditions. According to the latest official study conducted by the North American Conference of Associates and Religious (NACAR), in 2002, there were more than 27,000 lay associates in the United

States. NACAR estimates that today, this number is in the range of 35,000 to 40,000.

These new programs of lay association are of an astonishing reach and variety. But they do share a few characteristics. They are not officially recognized by Rome, and they entail no strict rules for daily life or obligations of membership, financial or otherwise. In some cases, associates support their religious communities only through their union with them in prayer; in others, associates are active participants in community functions and ministries.

Most lay associates today are women, but a host of communities of male religious also have associate programs. "Gender mixing" is also an interesting feature of many programs. Most men opt to affiliate with men's orders and women with women's, but in some cases, men's orders are open to women as associates, and women's orders to men.

A person interested in becoming a lay associate typically undergoes a process of formation lasting anywhere from six months to two years. During this time, he or she learns about the history and traditions of the community and may also be paired up with a professed member of the community who serves as a mentor. Upon completion of the formation period, the lay associate is initiated into the community through some form of commitment ceremony. Unlike their forebears and those today participating in the older traditions of lay oblates and third orders, lay associates typically make a temporary but renewable commitment of one to three years.

By and large, lay associates are just regular people, living in their own homes with their families and going to work every day. What distinguishes them, and leads them to make this special religious commitment, is a heartfelt "spiritual hunger" demanding a deeper, more formal outlet for their spiritual quest. And the benefits of association flow to each role—to the layperson and to the community alike. As one nun is reported to have commented, "Our associates assist us in our mission and bring our charism into the larger world." Another reflects, "The associates seem to value and see goodness in who we are (as religious) more than we see in ourselves."[*]

At the risk of relapsing into reciting a catalogue, let us again offer a brief sample—merely suggestive, entirely fragmentary—of the almost infinite possibilities. Some are of a lineage many centuries old; others are responses to new needs that only became visible during the past few decades. New ones are being born each day. God seems able to call up an almost unlimited number of intelligent and committed new leaders among His people in each new hour of need.

Lay Carmelites, Lay Dominicans, Secular Franciscans, the Oblates of St. Benedict, and the Norbertine Associates are representative of the older traditions.[†] Unlike the new programs of lay association, these are recognized by the Vatican as official orders within the Catholic Church.

Each of these groups characterizes its mission as contributing to the transformation of the secular world in its own distinctive way, through various manifestations of its particular charism. Each emphasizes the need to recognize in the very ordinary circumstances of daily life the presence of God and the many opportunities for receiving and sharing His grace. Unlike the contemporary movements, membership in these groups entails a more rigorous and lengthy period of study and spiritual formation. Upon completing this process, individuals make

---

[*] "Who's Following Orders? The Appeal of Religious Associates," *U.S. Catholic* (August 1, 1997).

[†] More detailed information, including discussion of the history, charisms, and formation processes of each, is available at the following websites. Lay Carmelites: www.laycarmelites.com. Lay Dominicans: www.3op.org. Secular Franciscans: www. nafra-sfo.org. Oblates of St. Benedict: www.osb.org. Norbertine Associates: http:// www.premontre.org/Publica/Vocations%20Page/@Voc-Laity.htm.

a permanent, lifelong commitment, though one still compatible with the normal human responsibilities of work and family.

Kathleen Norris is the author of two well-received books, *Dakota: A Spiritual Geography* and *The Cloister Walk*. Her story of searching for and finding spiritual fulfillment by becoming a Benedictine oblate is worthwhile reading for anyone considering this outlet for the lay vocation.

Other newer programs of lay association are the Associates of the Sisters of Providence of Saint Mary-of-the-Woods, Indiana.* Open to Catholic and non-Catholic women and men at least 18 years old, this program is grounded in the community's charism of "indomitable trust in God's Providence," exemplified most clearly in the life of the community's founder, St. Mother Theodore Guerin. After a program of "Spiritual Integration," formation, and discernment, associates make a one-year renewable commitment, during which time they participate in the life and mission of the community by means of common and mutual prayer, participation in reflection and prayer groups, retreats, and other spiritual and ministerial outreach.

Another is the Associates of the Franciscan Friars of the Renewal.† Founded in 1990, the associates are a group of laymen and laywomen who learn to follow Christ by studying the model of St. Francis of Assisi. They hold monthly group meetings in the South Bronx, where they gather for a day of prayer, service, and spiritual fellowship. On these days, service projects include cleaning, maintenance, and gardening at a local homeless shelter, sorting donated clothes, and preparing food baskets for the needy. Associates also attend monthly meetings for Bible study, Mass, and a potluck dinner, and they make annual retreats and plan biennial pilgrimages to holy sites.

---

* See http://www.spsmw.org.
† See www.franciscanfriars.com/welcome/lay_associates.htm.

The Missionaries of the Gospel of Life is the program of lay association with the group Priests for Life.* The founding of this community was inspired by the belief that those engaged in pro-life work would "be affirmed in what they are doing by their unity with other members." Individuals promise to make a lifetime commitment to minister to people in all facets of the pro-life movement through prayer, mutual spiritual support, and educational programs.

One last group to mention in our sample: the Basilian Lay Associates.† This international association of men and women emphasizes both personal spiritual formation and the development of community relationships. Members are encouraged to be active in their parishes and to participate in daily prayer, spiritual direction, monthly meetings, and an annual retreat. The Basilian community functions as an extended family of sorts, with group events such as liturgies and celebrations of anniversaries and other important events. All members of the Basilian community throughout the world are joined in unity through their prayers, communication, and personal meetings.

These are the more traditional forms of lay affiliation, whereby individuals associate themselves with already established religious orders and communities. But another category of new lay movements has popped up in recent decades. Several lay groups that focus on a highly developed sense of spirituality were given special Vatican recognition by John Paul II. These include Opus Dei, Regnum Christi, Comunione e Liberazione, Focolare, and the Community of St. Egidio. Working in harmony with the hierarchy of the Church, these organizations have nourished the spiritual life and activity of hundreds of

---

* See www.priestsforlife.org/missionary/about-us.htm.
† See www.basilian.org.

thousands of laypersons worldwide, and they continue to grow and be noticed.

Thus, looking around at the thriving possibilities for greater and greater lay commitment in our time is a little like standing beneath the dark Mediterranean sky under the seemingly millions of stars that captivated the imagination of young St. Augustine on the midnight sands of the African coast. They are of a dizzying vastness and variety.

CHAPTER 22

Single or Married—
Answering God's Call

"Let us not forget that the lay state has advantages and indeed sacrifices of its own. Religious vows are by no means the only form of heroism open to the Christian who is seeking holiness. The obligations of marriage are in fact often no less difficult than those of the cloister."
—THOMAS MERTON, *LIFE AND HOLINESS*

Closer to home—and, in fact, right within our homes—there is another powerful source for spiritual growth that has been commonly overlooked in guidebooks for the laity. Most spiritual writing in the Church has been done with the priestly and the religious, celibate life in view. There is an immense amount to be learned from that approach.

Still, it would be odd if God called most laypeople (about two-thirds) to married life and there were no special call to growth in the interior life by way of marital sex. It is not only celibacy that is a great teacher of self-knowledge (and it is that). So also is marital sex: it's so physical a feature of married life that we seldom think of its spiritual aspects. But it is a resource for forming a deeper interior life. It is rich in opportunity for reflection, rich in goads to honesty and self-reflection, rich in the lessons of how hard it is to live well an intimate life with a person of the opposite sex.

A full one-third of all laypeople are not called to married life—or, at least, not yet. Many are single and intend to remain single. That in itself is a distinctive vocation, with its own riches and stresses. When the vocation of a man or a woman is to be single (at least for a rather long time), there is still a significant difference between a layperson who is willing to marry, or open to marriage, or even wants to marry—and a person living a life consecrated to celibacy in the single-minded service of the Lord.

All single persons are bound to chastity—fidelity to the Lord in practicing no acts of sex outside marriage. In giving humans marital sex, the Creator gave them a very precious gift, in imitation of His own life: a communion of persons each distinct, and yet two made one in the act of joining bodies and souls in ways that are in principle the creation of new human life. But not all laypersons are called to married life. These too have a precious vocation.

God calls people to the single life for many reasons. Who knows for sure what are the reasons? In searching for God's reasons, we trust His kindliness, goodness, and sweetly solicitous wisdom, even when we do not understand. We keep our hearts and souls open and try to spread the caritas the Lord infuses into us, His own fiery love. We spread this distinctive divine love openly and fully to all those of His children He sends our way. There is a lovely openness that singles can show to others who are in need, a chaste and delightful love, the more trustworthy and more easily acceptable by those in need of disinterested, selfless love.

And joy. There is often a joy accessible to the single persons, precisely in their purity of heart, which they communicate to others without worry or preoccupation. The unmarried heart has its own special beauty, as all of us have experienced with marvel and wonderment. It radiates from relatives, friends, and even strangers. We all feel gratitude for the ways our lives are enriched by them. (Many of us point easily to the one in our family who is the "saint" holding the rest of us together, taking up duties essential for all of us.)

Those of us who are open to marriage nourish in ourselves, meanwhile, a terrible vulnerability. We are drawn by a bodily yearning, as well as a yearning of our spirits, for sexual unity with another person of the opposite gender. We pray often that Providence will send us the love we would embrace if it appeared. Any one of us "may meet a stranger, across a crowded room." Persons consecrated solely to God must greatly resist that natural desire of the heart. That is precisely what they have consciously and deliberately chosen, in order to keep the caritas within them open to all without sexual implications. Theirs is a love purely at the service of others: a beautiful gift of God, a potent sign of His living, infinite presence. Celibate love may be the most fruitful of all loves, in thousands of families and lives.

For the married person, however, the role of sexual life is quite different. In books, lectures, and articles—or so we have found it—a profound part of the sexual life has scarcely been mentioned. We mean the immense spiritual, emotional, and even bodily difficulties that must be experienced as two distinctive persons struggle to become one. None of us knows in advance how the many different energies and complexities of our own sexual being will function when the time comes—and particularly with this one chosen partner to whom we have committed our lives. We do not know in advance the complexities in this other opposite-gendered being. For it is not merely adapting to a different gender (this alone is hard enough) but to this one, utterly distinctive other. We are not marrying another gender; we are marrying another person.

It is one thing to feel the exciting and comforting energies of our changing bodies that unfold in marital sexual communion. But it is another to anticipate the associations of our own previous emotional histories in this exchange. Sex is by no means merely a physical coupling. It is that, and quite wonderfully. But it precipitates, as well, deep shifts in our own self-understanding and in our understanding of this mysterious other to whom we are so powerfully drawn.

Emotional chain reactions may be touched off—attractions, fears, alarms, vulnerabilities—that were totally unexpected. One person or the other may have been particularly "wounded" in an earlier relationship (Cupid shoots painful arrows). One partner may find it much harder than the other to let go, to plunge into the most vulnerable of unities. Egos may be hurt. Expectations may not for some time be fulfilled. It is not unusual for sex to be something of a dread, perhaps even for months or years. One can dread being a failure, letting that other person down, and unintentionally, without knowing it, inflicting a wound. "We always hurt the one we love."

Sexual life, in short, is an amazingly delicate, complicated, mystifying, constantly shifting long-term adventure, an unplanned voyage of discernment, fraught with hesitations and fears. It is fairly common that sex together becomes far more mutually satisfying, two more easily joining together in later years than in earlier. And G.K. Chesterton is right about the humor-laden trick the Creator has played in giving us human sexuality: a married couple is a four-legged animal, struggling to become one.

On the first page of the Bible, at the head of the Book, we are told that our Maker created both Adam and Eve—"man and woman He made them"—and made them, as a couple, "in the image of God He made them." In some profound way, the communion of man and woman is an image of the inner communion of God's own life.

It is quite true, as Pope John Paul II taught, that we humans are not divided into body and soul. Each of us learns, gradually, that our spirit fires every action of our body, and our body conditions every dimension of our souls. We are not divided into soul and body. The common expectation that we are is the source of immense mischief in marital sexual life. Our bodies affect every dimension of our souls down into their remotest mysteries, and our spirits intensify and enrich every nerve of our body.

Look at your hand: it is not out there, separate, physical. It is really not. Your whole spiritual energy is in it, in its sensitive touch, in its warm life. A marital caress is our souls talking, not just our flesh. It is a great failure in modern manuals of sexual advice (how many there are; how much dissatisfaction there must be!) that they attend mostly to the functions of our bodies. They almost wholly overlook our souls. And that is where the aches are.

Then there is the important matter of "coming down to earth." When I, Michael, was committed to celibacy as a young religious, preparing to be ordained a priest, it never occurred to me that in married life, one of the most difficult tasks would be finding privacy, time, space in which to enjoy sexual coupling. I guess I thought that would be easy. In real life, however, given hectic modern schedules, having children all around us in unpredictable need, with our diverse emotions not always at peace, not always ready to be attentive to each other—in real life, sexual acts turned out to be (after the honeymoon and the first childless months) a rare opportunity to be treasured. Good moments may need to be set in motion, almost "planned for," days in advance. It is not only the wife who must sometimes say,

"Not tonight, dear." Sometimes her husband will say, "I must finish this report" or "I've got to get a good sleep tonight, to be sharp at that trial." Human beings are immensely complex bundles of psychic history and insistent daily preoccupations. Before marriage, I never dreamed how two persons would be so nontransparent, and their lovemaking so dependent on ser- endipity, so unpredictable, so mystifying. At times, everything is glorious; at other times, disappointing.

Thus, the task of lovers in practicing "the theology of the body" is far more a matter of gift and contingency and nonlogi- cal discernment than theologians tend to think of. It is so darn complicated underneath its basic, primitive movements. It is a most amazing spiritual adventure. And teacher. And demander.

There is no point in being married if we do not sometimes feel woefully inadequate to how deep such a life is. There is no point in being married if you do not like to hear a spouse point out to you all the faults in yourself you would just as soon not hear about, at least not now. Marriage is the truth-telling insti- tution par excellence. A marriage cannot last on illusions.

The Catholic Church has not yet in its long history thought through the spiritual riches latent in marital sexual love. Lay- persons will one day need to do that. Here, though, the inter- est of all of us lies in how to become a more serious, joyous Christian. We seek some simple, solid exercises that help us to do so.

We said that the vocation of the laity differs from that of priests and nuns in its worldly responsibilities, first, and, second, in the centrality of sex and family to its spiritual life. In both these ways, lay life is a great teacher of honesty and realism.

Of course, it may be countered that the consecrated, celi- bate person's concentration on eternity and the world of grace teaches them too, though in a different sense, a searing realism. In the Final Vision toward which our lives are hurtling with alarming rapidity, in which we will stand before God as He is, all our equipment of perception will fail, and most of what once seemed so important to us will then seem as so much straw. It is the task of the ordained and the professed religious to lift our eyes to the eternal and lasting things. In that too lies a necessary honesty, an indispensable clarity of mind.

Yet there is also a third way in which lay life differs significantly from that of the specially consecrated to God. Laypersons through marriage and sex accept the responsibilities for placing a sound financial footing under the children that they bring into this world—for their health, for their rich and complicated education (in their faith as well as in their secular calling; in their moral, prayerful and cultural life as well as in their mastery of professional methods and techniques). To become learned Christian humanists, in a position to change the world, just as to become serious, mature, jovial Christians, children today require years of financial care.

Priests and nuns may live in comparative poverty, under vows of poverty, but for many of them, this does not mean a drop in their standard of living but a detachment from worldly cares so they might better serve the people God has committed to their care.

For the layperson, providing for a child's good upbringing—the best one can afford—can be an onerous, consuming, worrying task, however rich with satisfactions. A layperson can feel under significantly greater economic pressure and responsibility. Psychologically, at least, this difference in personal responsibility, although deliberately chosen and accepted by each, may alter dramatically the way in which laypersons see and experience economic reality.

So the differences are marked between the lives of laypersons and those especially consecrated to God as priests and religious. Small wonder, then, that the interior life of the two different vocations would now require new thinking that is clear, original, and solidly rooted in Catholic principles and experience.

Let us summarize the ways in which the internal struggles of marriage deepen our interior lives—the life, as they used to say, of the soul. By the very principles of the theology of marriage, the changes that affect our bodily lives so profoundly as those of marriage also effect just as deeply, maybe more so, changes—a deepening, a broadening—in the lives of our souls too. That is, each person is a single unity of body and soul together. Learning to keep all our energies and powers in harmony is a lifetime's work.

Those of us who have sworn on our own account to live the examined life are very lucky if we have spouses who also demand of us total honesty and self-examination. Wanting to live an honest, limpid, open life ourselves, we get far more training in the demands of those ambitions in our married lives than is usually noticed. In marriage, with a fearless spouse, there is no place to hide. Your spouse has reasons—even necessities—to puncture your illusions, and with even more zest than you do. For one thing, one partner's cherished self-illusions can make a marriage almost unbearable for the other. Hardly an honest word can be said.

There is a story, perhaps apocryphal, about Henry Kissinger and his wife. It seems that one evening, they arrived back in their apartment after yet another splendid party that gave an award to Mr. Kissinger as "one of the great men" of the century. Handing Nancy the martini he had just carefully mixed, Mr. Kissinger pondered aloud, "I vunder how many great men there are in a century?" Wherewith, swirling her martini gently, Mrs. Kissinger gave him that cold, long-suffering look only a wife can give, and replied, "One fewer than you think, Henry."

Marriage teaches irreplaceable lessons in spiritual honesty.

This may be one reason that so often, the Gospels and Epistles take usages and practices borrowed from married life to illuminate the relation God wants with humans. Jesus, the Groom, takes the whole Church as His Spouse. The great Song of Songs, along with the Book of Wisdom, lays out with great tenderness the life of a beloved wife and husband, as a guide to the love of God for humans. It goes without saying, finally, that the Lord knows what is in us, sees right through us, seeks to burn away our self-illusions, rather like the honesty-craving spouse.

Marriage is a great teacher of self-purification, of other-centeredness, of delicacy of perception, and especially of attentiveness to those easily missed little signals that light our path toward the real. Marriage is a great purifier of the soul.

CHAPTER 23

Teach All Nations!

"We see the value of all . . . vocations, rooted as they are in the new life received in the Sacrament of Baptism. In a special way [we] discover ever more fully the specific vocation of the laity, called 'to seek the Kingdom of God by engaging in temporal affairs and by ordering them according to the plan of God.' They 'have their own role to play in the mission of the whole people of God in the Church and in the world . . . by their work for the evangelization and the sanctification of people.'"
—POPE JOHN PAUL II, "AT THE BEGINNING
OF THE THIRD MILLENNIUM"

"You can discover Christ through adoration; you can discover Christ through retreats and experiences like that. But to discover Christ through service was something very different for me."

—FROM THE PROFILE OF ELIAS MOO

The lay vocation flames out from God's caritas, from the very energy of God's inner life. The lay vocation's full and proper target is not merely assisting around the altar and staffing the administrative and ministerial arms of a parish. That work is blessed and necessary. But it is not yet the real work of the Church.

The real work of the Church lies in bringing God's love to men and women everywhere, in every occupation, in every state of soul. An immense field of the apostolate lies simply within ranks after ranks of those baptized Catholics who do not practice. Do you realize that of the 63 million Catholics the census finds in the United States, only 18 million are in church each Sunday? Just to rekindle the sparks of caritas in members of our own families, among our friends, and among many already on our parish rolls would involve us in converting millions of those whom God loves back into friendship with Him.

That is not even to mention the millions upon millions of former Catholics who left the practice of their faith two or three generations ago and whose children no longer practice. Nor is it to mention perhaps as many as 10 million to 20 million American Catholics who for nourishment and belonging have turned to various other Christian denominations. These other denominations sometimes teach these Catholics to think more deeply about their faith, to read Scripture closely, and to feel more fully the force of loving Christ. They give satisfactions these millions have not found in their particular Catholic community.

While we honor the consciences of all those who seek God more faithfully, we are sometimes pained that these millions are not being nourished by the Body and Blood of Christ. We hurt that they no longer share the bond that makes all Christians, from the Church's origins and early centuries, at one with us today, eating of the same Body and Blood, glorying in the one same faith.

If every practicing Catholic in America, attending Mass on Sunday, were to make up a list of just three family members or friends who are lapsed Catholics and manage by positive efforts over a year or two to bring them back to the Body and Blood, the active Church in America would grow from 18 million to 72 million.

If, during the next five years, these 72 million each felt the inner impulsion of the fiery life of the Trinity within them and directed its radiance outward into the minds of one other American whom God sends their way, the love of Christ might then nourish 144 million souls, one in unity with all the ages and ages of martyrs, saints and holy ones since the beginning. If this outreach were repeated during the next five years, the number of Catholics in America would grow to 288 million.

Looked at that way, the job is not so difficult, is it?

Ask yourself, in your lifetime, have you brought even one person into the embrace of the Trinity Who made that person for His love?

What would it be like if by the time one came to die, the number of friends one had brought to the Lord were 10 or more? All these would be friends forever in the Kingdom of the Lord. All these would be, even in this life, far happier people than they had been before. All these would be spreading God's love outward to the whole human race. Then the world would be shot through with that electronic band of "humble charity" that Dostoevsky called the most powerful force on earth.

Christian faith comes by hearing—one person at a time, one voice and one ear at a time. It comes person to person. It comes heart to heart. Do not scorn the humble situations of life—the very friends we now live with, our neighbors and other daily contacts. We can touch each of them with a smile whose backstory is that God loves them though us. Think of yourself in every situation as the bearer of God's love to this person (not some other, but the one God has now placed in front of you). Try to see what God loves in this person, even if you just don't see it.

Sister Gervase once told Michael in the seventh grade, "The trouble with the world is that people just don't share enough compliments. When you see something good or beautiful or well done, just tell people. You will lift their spirits and give them a shot of love good for the whole day, and maybe more. If you say to someone that they have a very dignified and pleasing walk, they will enjoy their own walking the whole rest of their lives. Tell people what gifts they have." These little things, she said, lighten the world.

God's love is made up of chains of humble little things.

The lay vocation is to change the world. That is, to inflame it with more of God's humble love, considerate and noticing love. Moreover, experience shows that quiet intensity matters. If you allow God's caritas to flood through you, as He longs for it to do, that adds eternal, divine significance to the tiny deeds you do. It gives them 10 times, a hundred times, a million times more divine power. For it is no longer you who love but God loving in you. And He rejoices to work through the humble, small things of this world far more than the grand. That is why He chooses you.

Be not afraid. Our God loves incarnation. He likes to reach human beings through the flesh. Now, today, we the living Body of Christ must be His arms and legs and hands, His voice, His sympathetic ear, His immense capacity for empathy, His generosity of spirit, His "disponibility"—that is, His ability to make Himself available to whoever needs Him, for however long.

God has made Himself dependent on us, His poor and humble laypeople. We are the bodily expressions of His infinite caritas. We are His carriers. We are His existing, current apostles. Without us, not much will get done. Through us, much more than we could possibly do alone, He will be able to do.

CHAPTER 24

To Rebuild All
Things in Christ

"A true apostle looks for opportunities to announce Christ by words addressed either to nonbelievers with a view to leading them to faith, or to the faithful with a view to instructing, strengthening them and encouraging them to a more fervent life."

—THE COUNCIL FATHERS OF VATICAN II,
APOSTOLICAM ACTUOSITATEM

"Are we being humble? Are we willing to serve? Are we willing to be the messengers of God?"

—FROM THE PROFILE OF ELIAS MOO

The prayer Jesus taught us is not that we should each have beautiful inner lives. It is that the Kingdom of His Father will come, on earth as it is in Heaven. We are to preach the Gospel to all nations. Our motto ought to be one of St. Paul's, as it was of Pope Pius X (the pope who allowed and encouraged daily Communion): *Instaurare omnia in Christo*. The usual translation of that line is "to restore all things in Christ." But we think that *instaurare* is better expressed by something like "to rebuild the foundations in Christ," or simply "to rebuild all things in Christ." In other words, not exactly as nature grounds things, but better than that, from a higher elevation than that, to refound all things in Christ. To make all things new.

So Christians are given an unusually high mission in the world: to bring out the better possibilities in everything, to reshape all things in the image and vitality and energy of Christ. Christianity typically works very slowly in history, not a little like yeast in dough—silently, from within, transformatively. Making dull, heavy dough more expansive, lighter, tastier. Transforming it from within.

The central mission of the Gospels is to transform each baptized person into another Christ and also to transform the City of Man (whose inner dynamic is egotism, self-pleasuring, and the lust for power over others) into the City of God. That is to say, it is to redirect life from within, from its good natural goals to the even better—unimaginably better—goals laid out in the Gospels.

In this way, grace does not cancel out human nature. Grace roots itself within human nature and lifts its trajectory, with infinite patience and very long time horizons. The purpose of the Gospels is not only to reform society but also to bring home to all individual souls, one by one, that they are called to a higher vocation than they have ever known. Their new vocation is caritas, to live by the higher law that Jesus Christ introduces into their lives, not just for their private and individual benefit but to lift all other human things higher, including societies, states, nations. It is to infuse all institutions with the spirit of the caritas poured out into their own lives by baptism and the other sacraments.

It is important to put first things first. It is individual persons whom God calls out. It is human persons whom He tries to transform into living images of Himself. It is in individual humans that He infuses the fire of His own inner life. He calls them and transforms them no matter what kind of society they live in.

Still, the purpose of calling human individuals is so they might rebuild the institutions of this earth, so they might better stimulate in individuals and families that love of God and love of neighbor that together constitute the highest goal of human society.

While this short introduction to the lay life is aimed primarily at deepening the inner lives of the new sort of Catholic layperson in this new world, it would be wrong to leave it at that point. We need to utter at least a few words about how to seed the transformative power of that inner life into the dynamics of our current, contingent, fragile social life—into its institutions and into its modes of operation. Our call is to save our own souls but also to suffuse throughout the institutions of our time the same principles of caritas that daily reshape our own inner lives. This is where the interior life of the layperson meets the exterior life.

The world may be pluralistic, and there may be beautiful features in every culture and society. But the special call given to Judaism and Christianity, among all other religions, is to inspire new societies whose focal points are the human person, made in the image of God and animated by God's own love within, and to inspire the whole human community.

There is a special dynamic force in Jewish and Christian cultures. These are pre-eminently the cultures of liberty, fraternity, and equality under the law. These are the cultures expressive of the image of God at their very center. The God Who is both person and community. The Liberator, Who assigns responsibility to each while calling all together into international solidarity—that is, into a City of freedom, responsibility, and love.

The God Who is not arbitrary, unpredictable Will—the will
to power—but the God Who is Logos, that is, Understanding
(Insight) and Law.

As Lord Acton pointed out in his notes for his massive *History of Liberty* (uncompleted at his death), the history of individual and social freedom in human history is coincident with
the history of Judaism and Christianity. Where these two religions go, a distinctive set of institutions protecting liberty, and
distinctive institutions nourishing both the human person and
the human community, spring up like blossoms, flowers, and
fresh green grasses in April and May.

In our time, one of the key terms for describing how God
works in history (that is, the social agenda of Christian faith)
has been *social justice*. Nearly always, though, this term is used
badly, or at least imprecisely, even by active Catholics, even by
learned bishops. Not everyone has yet grasped its distinctively
Christian bearing. Out of habit and laziness, many Christians
tend to think of social justice as common to social democracy
and even socialism itself. They think that social justice means
supporting state programs to care for the needs of the poor.
They link social justice to statism.

In this historical context, the term *social justice* emerged with
a specific meaning, different from those we considered earlier.
Social justice names a new set of habits and abilities that need
to be learned, perfected, and passed on. In other words, social
justice is a new virtue with very powerful social consequences.
It is the virtue of forming associations and other "mediating
institutions."

Social justice is called "social" for two reasons. First, its aim
or purpose is to improve the common good of society at large,
outside the family especially, perhaps on a national scale or an
international scale, but certainly on a range of social institutions

nearer home. A village or neighborhood may need a new well, or a new school, or even a church. Workers may need to form a union and to unite with other unions. Since the cause of the wealth of nations is invention and intellect, new colleges and universities need to be founded. Wealth now comes primarily through ideas, not land.

In America, the new immigrants formed athletic clubs for the young; for the adult males, social clubs to play checkers, cards, or horseshoes; for the women, associations to tend to the needs of neighbors. Since many of the men worked as many as 12 hours a day in the mines or the mills, the women conducted much of the social business of the neighborhoods in political and civic circles. The immigrants formed insurance societies and other associations of mutual help to care for one another in cases of injury and premature death. In a word, Tocqueville was correct when he called the voluntary forming of associations by citizens, to meet their own social needs, "the first law of democracy."*

But this new virtue was called social for a second reason. Not only is its end social but so also are its constitutive practices. The practice of the virtue of social justice consists in learning new skills of cooperation and association with others in order to accomplish ends that no one individual could achieve on his own. At one pole, this new virtue is a social protection against atomic individualism, while at the other pole, it protects considerable civic space from the direct custodianship of the state.

It is a good thing that the popes thought of this definition as ideologically neutral. Social justice is practiced both by those on the left and those on the right. (There is more than one way

---

* Alexis de Toqueville, *Democracy in America* (New York: Vintage Books, 1945), 189.

to imagine the future good of society.) Humans of all persuasions do well to master the new social virtue that assists them in defining and in working with others toward their own vision of that good.

In this book, we have concentrated on the amazing growth in the number of laypeople assisting in parishes and other institutions of the Catholic Church. We have tried to set out practical ways for entering into the new interior life required by those who want to perform their new Church duties in the spirit and with the virtues of Jesus Christ. What is the point of performing as a minister of the Gospels if one does not live the life of the Gospels? And how is that to be done in the 21st century?

We are well aware that there is one other crucial prong of the whole argument that we have barely touched on, namely, that the primary duty of the new laity is to carry the Gospel to all nations—to move outward, to change and to evangelize a world that was made for liberty, peace, justice, and love for one another.

This duty is not intended to be utopian. It is intended to begin now, with small steps, one person to another, in plodding practice more than in soaring theory. The role of the new laity consists also in transforming the world through carrying the Holy Spirit and the Spirit of Christ into its every nook and cranny, into every calling, into all the activities of the workaday world—into business, law, education, nongovernmental organizations, construction, manufacturing, advertising, communications, the arts, the military, medicine, and all the other activities through which ordinary people give glory to God in their everyday lives.

This is the challenge given to all laypeople by the late Pope John Paul II: to take up the precious work of implanting the yeast of the Gospels into every work of human hands and heart, to plunge ourselves into the rough texture of the yet-unfinished world.